CONTENTS

PROLOGUE

For most of my life I have been telling Bible stories to children. I've told the historical accounts of God's people and the miracles the LORD worked time and time again. I love God's Word. I love each and every historical account. I could tell them all day long and in my sleep! They are the most riveting and inspiring stories ever...and most importantly they are the foundation of our confidence of the LORD'S sovereignty, His great power, and His great love for humanity.

I just never imagined that I would see these very Bible stories that I've been retelling all my life, playing out before my very eyes. When I first realized we were experiencing the Book of Revelation, I began to ask the LORD to help me understand and unravel the knots of lies we had been told about End Times.

We had been misled and frightened to pieces so that many believers are hiding under the bed and have their bags packed to escape earth. Obviously that's exactly where the mafia cabal criminal Deep State Beast in Revelation wants believers to be, instead of in the fight exposing their crimes. But I am here to tell you this is the End Times for them and 1,000 years of peace <u>on earth</u> for humanity!

So get out from under the bed and let's join the fight. This book is not specifically about Revelation or End Times. If you want the true decode of Revelation, check out my Bestseller, *"End Times and 1000 Years of Peace."* You can also check out my other Bestseller, *"End Times - Major Clues from Minor Prophets"* to see how the LORD promised through the Minor Prophets that this day would come, when humanity would wake up and cast out these evildoers. And the Minor Prophets told us about our great victory just up ahead!

This book has been on my heart to write since I woke up just before President Trump was elected…the first time. I have been telling these Bible stories for so long, and now I get to tell how they are being fulfilled in our day! We as humanity are living out and experiencing these 17 historical accounts from God's Word. How cool for the LORD to create this amazing Biblical road map for us!

You will love it!

Remember Moses leading the people out of Egypt and parting the Red Sea so the Israelites could escape Pharaoh and the Egyptian army?

Remember young David killing Goliath?

Remember Daniel in the lions' den?

And Shadrach, Meschach, and Abednego in the fiery furnace?

Remember how the LORD used Joseph to save the world from famine?

And how Elijah destroyed the prophets of Baal?

What about Samson bringing down the columns and destroying all the "elite" Philistines?

And Deborah, Yael, Joshua, Gideon, and Esther?

These Biblical accounts are not just ancient history. They are happening all around us! Different names. Different locations. But each story is being fulfilled in our day as we wage this great Battle of Armageddon!

Our victory is sure.

There is no reason to fear.

The only thing we must do is redouble our efforts and charge into the battle just as our forefathers did. The Millennial Reign of Christ on earth, where the righteous will inherit the earth, is just over that next hill. Come with me on a journey through the Old Testament, as we look at the current events in the light of God's Word. I hope you enjoy this book and the LORD uses it to encourage and embolden you as never before.

In Jesus name.

Amen

If you would like to learn more about how what we are experiencing is literally Biblical and join us in the fight for humanity, check out *FreedomForce.LIVE.*

1 NOAH - THE FLOOD WASHED THEM ALL AWAY

I don't know about you, but I don't really consider the Biblical account of Noah and the flood a very good bedtime story for kids. There are a lot of shocking stories in God's Word, but I'd say the flood that destroyed all of humanity except for eight people, would be number one.

Noah and his family, a total of eight people, were literally the only righteous people on earth. They were the only ones who had not been taken captive by demons who lived in them and controlled them. That sounds outrageous, but that is what God's Word says. All of humanity had been deceived into worshiping demons. No wonder the LORD regretted creating man.

Our LORD Jesus told us End Times would be like the days of Noah when the people would be enjoying parties and wouldn't know what hit them until the flood came and washed them all away. Our LORD Jesus was telling us the at the End Times there would be a "reenactment" of Noah's flood.

MATTHEW 24

37 "When the Son of Man returns, it will be like it was in Noah's day.

38 In those days before the flood, the people were enjoying banquets and parties and weddings right up to the time Noah entered his boat.

39 People didn't realize what was going to happen until the flood came and swept them all away. That is the way it will be when the Son of Man comes."

But there is one difference I want to point out. The LORD promised with the rainbow that He would never destroy **humanity** again with a flood.

GENESIS 8

*21 "I will never again curse the ground because of the human race, even though everything they think or imagine is bent toward evil from childhood. I will never again destroy **all living things**."*

What was the LORD saying? <u>He was NOT saying</u> that He lost His temper and destroyed humanity in a fit of rage, and would never lose His temper again.

<u>He was saying demons would never again be able to take over humanity</u>.

The LORD would cause major changes on earth so demons would not be able take possession of the vast majority of humanity ever again. The people had been almost helpless to overcome the demons' trickery. We had to see what would happen to humanity if the LORD left us to our own strength against the demons.

It was NOT GOOD.

The promise was that the LORD would never destroy <u>humanity</u> again. He would never again need to destroy humanity, because He would give us the power to overcome the demons. Jesus said that in the End Times the flood would wash **them** away...as in **wash away the <u>remaining</u> demon worshipers.**

The problem Noah faced was that many of the people had become possessed by demons dwelling within them and acting through them. "The wickedness became great on the earth continually," because people were operating under the influence of demons. Demons "possessed" the people and caused terrible wickedness on the earth.

For Noah and his family to stand against the tide of that evil culture and the demons' trickery took superhuman strength. The only ones who successfully exhibited that superhuman strength were Noah and his family. If the satan worshipers killed Noah and his family, the entire earth would be under the control of satan. So the LORD told Noah He was going to take drastic measures. He told Noah to build an ark because He would rescue Noah and his family, but the rest of humanity – the demon worshipers - would be destroyed in a flood.

Noah preached every day, trying desperately to reason with the people. But they wouldn't listen. When people are literally possessed by a demon they cannot listen to reason. They are under strong delusion and are deceived.

Finally the day came when the ark was completed. The Lord told Noah to put two of each kind of animal inside the ark. Once they were all safely inside, the LORD closed the door and the rain and floodwaters started. Just as the LORD said, every man, woman, and child died except for those who were inside the ark.

The good news is that the LORD had a plan that would ultimately flip the script entirely. Instead of only a small percentage of humanity who worshiped the LORD, one day there would only be a small percentage of humanity who worshiped demons.

Did you catch that?

That is VERY IMPORTANT.

Instead of only a small percentage of humanity who worshiped the LORD, one day there would only be a small percentage of humanity who worshiped demons.

That is where we are on God's timeline.

Yes. A lot of people are caught up in sin and are deceived. But most people do not literally worship demons. Most people can't even imagine someone allowing demons to dwell within them, much less consider doing such a thing themselves!

People are stressed.

People are angry.

People have been tricked into believing many lies.

People have made some terrible mistakes and sinned against the LORD.

But most people do not worship demons or have demons control them.

How was humanity able to overcome falling into satan's trap again?

First, we have been working toward that goal of ridding the world of demon worshipers since our Lord Jesus issued the Great Commission.

> MATTHEW 28
>
> *19 "Therefore, go and make disciples of all the nations, baptizing them in the name of the Father and the Son and the Holy Spirit.*
>
> *20 Teach these new disciples to obey all the commands I have given you. And be sure of this: I am with you always, even to the end of the age."*

One of our LORD Jesus' commands was to go and make disciples of all the nations and to baptize them in the **Holy Spirit**. In other words…fill everyone on earth with the Holy Spirit rather than demonic spirits. And, with all of humanity's faults, most are not demon worshipers! Mission Accomplished!

And something amazing happened when our LORD Jesus died on the cross and rose from the dead. We know He paid for sin with His atoning blood, so our sins are forgiven. When Jesus ascended to the right hand of the Father, He gave humanity an amazing gift. He sent the Holy Spirit to dwell within us. This was a huge shift from what humanity had experienced before. Now we experience the power of the Holy Spirit to overcome the temptations of the demons. The power of the Holy Spirit gives us a fighting chance. And this amazing gift was purchased by the atoning sacrifice of our LORD Jesus Christ on the cross. This is what Jesus told the disciples.

JOHN 14

17 "He is the Holy Spirit, who leads into all truth. The world cannot receive him, because it isn't looking for him and doesn't recognize him.

*But you know him, because he lives with you now and **later will be in you**."*

Notice our Lord Jesus said the Holy Spirit lived *with* them but later would be **IN** them. That's a huge difference as far as us having the power to overcome the dark forces of evil.

After our LORD Jesus rose from the dead, He appeared to His disciples and He breathed on them...

As He breathed on them He said "Receive the Holy Spirit."

Imagine that.

The LORD Jesus breathing on you...and you receive the Holy Spirit.

The Comforter.

The Guide into all truth.

The One who gives us the same power that was in Christ to raise Him from the dead! POW!

ROMANS 8

5 "Those who live according to the flesh have their minds set on what the flesh desires; but those who live in accordance with the Spirit have their minds set on what the Spirit desires.

6 The mind governed by the flesh is death, but the mind governed by the Spirit is life and peace.

7 The mind governed by the flesh is hostile to God; it does not submit to God's law, nor can it do so.

8 Those who are in the realm of the flesh cannot please God.

9 You, however, are not in the realm of the flesh but are in the realm of the Spirit, if indeed the Spirit of God lives in you. And if anyone does not have the Spirit of Christ, they do not belong to Christ.

10 But if Christ is in you, then even though your body is subject to death because of sin, the Spirit gives life because of righteousness.

11 And if the Spirit of him who raised Jesus from the dead is living in you, he who raised Christ from the dead will also give life to your mortal bodies because of his Spirit who lives in you.

12 Therefore, brothers and sisters, we have an obligation—but it is not to the flesh, to live according to it. 13 For if you live according to the flesh, you will die; but if by the Spirit you put to death the misdeeds of the body, you will live."

We have power over sin, because the same Spirit that raised Christ from the dead lives in us!

This is the beautiful account of Jesus breathing on His disciples to receive the Holy Spirit.

JOHN 20

19 "That Sunday evening the disciples were meeting behind locked doors because they were afraid of the Jewish leaders. Suddenly, Jesus was standing there among them! "Peace be with you," he said.

20 As he spoke, he showed them the wounds in his hands and his side. They were filled with joy when they saw the Lord!

21 Again he said, "Peace be with you. As the Father has sent me, so I am sending you."

22 Then he breathed on them and said, "Receive the Holy Spirit."

Our LORD Jesus had told the disciples to stay together in Jerusalem, until they received the promised gift from Heaven. And on the Day of Pentecost, Day 50 after the Resurrection and the Counting of the Omer, Jesus sent the Holy Spirit, as He had promised. Here is the account:

ACTS 2

1 "On the day of Pentecost all the believers were meeting together in one place.

2 Suddenly, there was a sound from heaven like the roaring of a mighty windstorm, and it filled the house where they were sitting.

3 Then, what looked like flames or tongues of fire appeared and settled on each of them.

4 And everyone present was filled with the Holy Spirit and began speaking in other languages, as the Holy Spirit gave them this ability.

5 At that time there were devout Jews from every nation living in Jerusalem.

6 When they heard the loud noise, everyone came running, and they were bewildered to hear their own languages being spoken by the believers.

7 They were completely amazed. "How can this be?" they exclaimed. "These people are all from Galilee,

8 and yet we hear them speaking in our own native languages!

9 Here we are—Parthians, Medes, Elamites, people from Mesopotamia, Judea, Cappadocia, Pontus, the province of Asia,

10 Phrygia, Pamphylia, Egypt, and the areas of Libya around Cyrene, visitors from Rome

11 (both Jews and converts to Judaism), Cretans, and Arabs.

And we all hear these people speaking in our own languages about the wonderful things God has done!"

12 They stood there amazed and perplexed. "What can this mean?" they asked each other.

13 But others in the crowd ridiculed them, saying, "They're just drunk, that's all!"

14 Then Peter stepped forward with the eleven other apostles and shouted to the crowd, "Listen carefully, all of you, fellow Jews and residents of Jerusalem! Make no mistake about this.

15 These people are not drunk, as some of you are assuming. Nine o'clock in the morning is much too early for that.

16 No, what you see was predicted long ago by the prophet Joel:

17 'In the last days,' God says,
'I will pour out my Spirit upon all people.
Your sons and daughters will prophesy.
Your young men will see visions,
and your old men will dream dreams.

18 In those days I will pour out my Spirit
even on my servants—men and women alike—
and they will prophesy.

19 And I will cause wonders in the heavens above
and signs on the earth below—
blood and fire and clouds of smoke.

20 The sun will become dark
and the moon will turn blood red
before that great and glorious day of the Lord arrives.
21 But everyone who calls on the name of the Lord.
will be saved.'"

The Holy Spirit came to indwell everyone who called upon the name of the LORD in repentance and faith. THAT is what has changed humanity. Because of the indwelling of the Holy Spirit we have the power to stand against the schemes of the spiritual forces as Ephesians 6 says:

EPHESIANS 6

10 "Be strong in the Lord and in his mighty power.

11 Put on all of God's armor so that you will be able to stand firm against all strategies of the devil.

12 For we are not fighting against flesh-and-blood enemies, but against evil rulers and authorities of the unseen world, against mighty powers in this dark world, and against evil spirits in the heavenly places.

*13 Therefore, **put on every piece of God's armor so you will be able to <u>resist the enemy</u> in the time of evil. Then after the battle you will still be <u>standing firm</u>.***

***14 <u>Stand your ground,</u>** putting on the belt of truth and the body armor of God's righteousness.*

15 For shoes, put on the peace that comes from the Good News so that you will be fully prepared.

16 In addition to all of these, hold up the shield of faith to stop the fiery arrows of the devil.

17 Put on salvation as your helmet, and take the sword of the Spirit, which is the word of God.

18 Pray in the Spirit at all times and on every occasion. Stay alert and be persistent in your prayers for all believers everywhere."

Believers in Christ are enabled to stand against the enemy by the power of the Holy Spirit. Most of the people who lived during Noah's day could not overcome the demons, but by the power of the Holy Spirit, WE CAN. The blessing of the Holy Spirit has caused the vast majority of humanity to recoil at the very notion of demonic possession!

The LORD Jesus told His disciples to go into all the world and preach the gospel...to fill the earth with people who walk with Him and are filled with the Holy Spirit. There is no other explanation for how humanity is rising up against the tyrants peacefully and patriotically. The only explanation is that we are filled with the Holy Spirit and are being led by Him.

No doubt the worldwide flood is being "reenacted" in our day. Only this time, we will see the fulfillment as our LORD Jesus told us "the flood will wash **them** (the demon worshipers) all away."

2 JACOB - AT DAWN I WILL WIN!

GENESIS 15

5 "Then the Lord took Abram outside and said to him, "Look up into the sky and count the stars if you can. That's how many descendants you will have!"

6 And Abram believed the Lord, and the Lord counted him as righteous because of his faith."

GENESIS 17

1 "When Abram was ninety-nine years old, the Lord appeared to him and said, "I am El-Shaddai—'God Almighty.' Serve me faithfully and live a blameless life.

2 I will make a covenant with you, by which I will guarantee to give you countless descendants."

3 At this, Abram fell face down on the ground. Then God said to him,

4 "This is my covenant with you: I will make you the father of a multitude of nations!

5 What's more, I am changing your name. It will no longer be Abram. Instead, you will be called Abraham, for you will be the father of many nations.

6 I will make you extremely fruitful. Your descendants will become many nations, and kings will be among them!

7 "I will confirm my covenant with you and your descendants after you, from generation to generation. This is the everlasting covenant: I will always be your God and the God of your descendants after you.

8 And I will give the entire land of Canaan, where you now live as a foreigner, to you and your descendants. It will be their possession forever, and I will be their God."

This the LORD's Covenant promise to Abraham, which has been confirmed in every generation since. Ultimately those who have the faith of Abraham will possess the entire land, forever. In other words, the **righteous will rule the earth.** We are witnessing Abraham's descendants taking possession of the earth. Truly. Here's where it began.

Because of Abraham's covenant with God, Abraham is the Father of faith. Every major religion has its roots in Abraham. That should be a great unifying truth! But the true history has been manipulated by false teachers to keep us divided. Imagine that.

The LORD promised to bless the world through Abraham, and no doubt that promise has been confirmed in every generation. Abraham had the miracle son, Isaac, when he was 99 years old. How's that for a miracle baby? Then Isaac married Rebekah and they had twins when Isaac was 62. Kinda pushing it! That is where we pick up our story, and we start to see how God's promise is being fulfilled in our day!

GENESIS 25

21 "Isaac pleaded with the Lord on behalf of his wife, because she was unable to have children. The Lord answered Isaac's prayer, and Rebekah became pregnant with twins.

22 But the two children struggled with each other in her womb. So she went to ask the Lord about it. "Why is this happening to me?" she asked.

*23 And the Lord told her, "**The sons in your womb will become two nations. From the very beginning, the two nations will be rivals. One nation will be stronger than the other; and your older son will serve your younger son.**"*

24 And when the time came to give birth, Rebekah discovered that she did indeed have twins!

25 The first one was very red at birth and covered with thick hair like a fur coat. So they named him Esau.

26 Then the other twin was born with his hand grasping Esau's heel. So they named him Jacob.

Rebekah could actually feel the two children fighting insider her womb! So moms, if your kids argue, you're in good company! Basically inside of Rebekah was not two nations like we usually think of nations. The modern church has watered-down the truth about Esau. Think of the battle between good and evil. The Lord promised that the older (Evil Esau) would serve the younger (Jacob/Israel). The New World Order demon worshipers represent the "nation" of Evil Esau. Believers all over the world represent the "nation" of Jacob/Israel. We have continued to grow and strengthen, but the Esau tyrants have always found a way to rule over us. It's been one epic struggle since the twins were in Rebekah's womb! But now, the promise is being fulfilled, "The older (Esau) will serve the younger (Jacob/Israel)." In other words, righteousness will fill the earth, and the evil will be outta here!

Rebekah's sons grew up side by side, but it was obvious that Esau was a selfish egotistical braggart who cared nothing for the blessings that flowed through Abraham and Isaac. But Jacob, on the other hand, wanted that blessing. I'm sure Rebekah had told him that blessing would be his. And that was foremost in his mind.

Jacob took the opportunity to buy the birthright from Esau for a bowl of stew. And Esau sold it! Whatever you think of that exchange, it shows Esau's utter disdain for that incomparable and priceless blessing, and how much Jacob desired the blessing of Abraham and Isaac.

The Book of Jasher even records that Abraham wanted the blessing to go to Jacob.

True to form, Esau did not keep his word, and when the time came for Isaac to give his blessing, Esau was going to have his cake and eat it too! Or have his stew, in this case. But while Esau was out hunting in preparation for the blessing ceremony, Jacob beat Esau to the punch! Here is the blessing Jacob received from Esau.

GENESIS 27

28 "From the dew of heaven
and the richness of the earth,
may God always give you abundant harvests of grain
and bountiful new wine.
29 May many nations become your servants,
and may they bow down to you.
May you be the master over your brothers,
and may your mother's sons bow down to you.
All who curse you will be cursed,
and all who bless you will be blessed."

Jacob wanted the blessing of Abraham and Isaac, AND HE GOT IT!

Many nations will become your servants. In other words, may Jacob rule the earth in righteousness. Truth is, if demon worshipers rule the earth, humanity wouldn't last a generation. Just look what happened in Noah's day! But if the righteous rule, the people flourish! Thank the LORD Jacob tricked Esau and got the blessing! But then Jacob had to run for his life! Esau was mad…and he's STILL MAD!

This is the blessing leftovers Esau received.

GENESIS 27

38 "Esau pleaded, "But do you have only one blessing? Oh my father, bless me, too!" Then Esau broke down and wept.

39 Finally, his father, Isaac, said to him,

"You will live away from the richness of the earth,
and away from the dew of the heaven above.
40 You will live by your sword,
and you will serve your brother.
But when you decide to break free,
you will shake his yoke from your neck."

Esau wanted to rule over Jacob. The evil-doer wanted to rule over the righteous. But the LORD would not allow it. Check out verse 40.

GENESIS 27

40 "You will live by your sword, and you will serve your brother."

You know that chaps Esau's hide to this day! He and his "descendants" are always fighting because they refuse law and order. Esau's descendants always want their lawless ways! The New World Order (NWO) cabal has followed in Esau's steps, and Esau followed in Cain's steps. Cain and Abel were Adam and Eve's first two sons. But Cain killed his brother Abel, because Abel was righteous. Cain wanted to be free of Abel's yoke. Cain didn't achieve freedom...only greater bondage. This was the curse on Cain. Even today, we talk about "Razing Cain." But it has a double meaning. Razing as in "leveling" Cain. We are bringing judgment and destruction on all the works of Cain since the first murder.

GENESIS 4

10 "But the LORD said, "What have you done? Listen! Your brother's blood cries out to me from the ground! 11 Now you are cursed and banished from the ground, which has swallowed your brother's blood.

12 No longer will the ground yield good crops for you, no matter how hard you work! From now on you will be a homeless wanderer on the earth."

That same judgment is on Esau in this strange verse.

GENESIS 27 KJV

*40 "and it shall come to pass when thou shalt have **the dominion,** that thou shalt break his yoke from off thy neck."*

The NWO desperately wants dominion. And not consequences. It is not a coincidence that the election machines are by a company name DOMINION.

This is how they have taken dominion…literally *stolen* dominion over us! But notice it says "thou shalt break his yoke from off thy neck." Initially that sounds like they will break free from the righteous. But what happens when the evildoers are allowed to do whatever they please? They destroy themselves and each other! And that is what we will see in other Bible stories being fulfilled, like the Battle of Jehoshaphat and the Battle of Gideon. And we are seeing that happen with the New World Order. Their lust for power and money has exposed them. Their arrogance has exposed them. They got sloppy because they figured they would never get caught. They have allowed their cronies to literally get away with murder, and they punished the righteous. And that will be their undoing, as prophecied.

DANIEL 8

23 "At the end of their rule, when their sin is at its height…"

25 "He will take on the Prince of princes in battle, but he will be broken, <u>though not by human power.</u>"

But now let's get back to the blessings of Jacob! Jacob literally ran to Beth El – which means the House of God. And he ran right into God! Jacob wanted the blessing. And that is exactly what he got! Beth El is where Jacob found the "Stone of Destiny" also known as "Jacob's Pillar." Here is the blessing Jacob received on top of Beth El.

GENESIS 28

10 "Meanwhile, Jacob left Beersheba and traveled toward

Haran.

11 At sundown he arrived at a good place to set up camp and stopped there for the night. Jacob found a stone to rest his head against and lay down to sleep.

12 As he slept, he dreamed of a stairway that reached from the earth up to heaven. And he saw the angels of God going up and down the stairway.

13 At the top of the stairway stood the Lord, and he said, "I am the Lord, the God of your grandfather Abraham, and the God of your father, Isaac. The ground you are lying on belongs to you. I am giving it to you and your descendants.

14 Your descendants will be as numerous as the dust of the earth! They will spread out in all directions—to the west and the east, to the north and the south. And all the families of the earth will be blessed through you and your descendants.

15 What's more, I am with you, and I will protect you wherever you go. One day I will bring you back to this land. I will not leave you until I have finished giving you everything I have promised you."

16 Then Jacob awoke from his sleep and said, "Surely the Lord is in this place, and I wasn't even aware of it!"

17 But he was also afraid and said, "What an awesome place this is! It is none other than the house of God, the very gateway to heaven!""

Just as Jacob wanted he received the blessing of his grandfather Abraham and his father Isaac!

GENESIS 28

13 "I am the Lord, the God of your grandfather Abraham, and the God of your father, Isaac. The ground you are lying on belongs to you. I am giving it to you and your descendants.

14 Your descendants will be as numerous as the dust of the earth!"

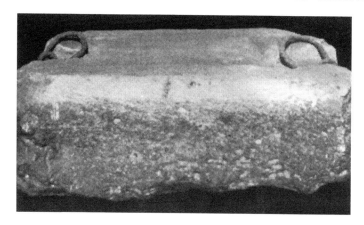

This blessing is not about dirt or land. This blessing is about having righteousness on the earth. This blessing is about who will rule the earth...the righteous or the wicked. And Jacob received the confirmation of that blessing, right at the doorway to Heaven! He knew the LORD was leading him and would fulfill His promise through him. He didn't know how long it would take for the promise to be fulfilled though!

Doesn't it seem as if the LORD was being repetitive? Jacob needed to be reminded that the LORD would bless his family, and protect them from attacks from all sides. We need that reminder too! And we need the LORD to be repetitive! Jacob miraculously received the blessing of Abraham and Isaac, and we are part of that wonderful family by faith.

The LORD told Jacob/Israel three times that He would be with him, and he would receive the blessings promised to Abraham and Issac...the blessings that the righteous would have more descendants than stars in the sky and sand on the seashore.

This promise was not only for Jacob/Israel, but for **all** his descendants. And the Bible is clear that those who have the same faith as Abraham <u>are children of Abraham</u>.

That is **us**! God's promises are for **us**!

GALATIANS 3

7 "The real children of Abraham, then, are those who put their faith in God."

Believers are true Israelites. Some by progeny and some by adoption. Bloodline is of no use without having the same faith in God as Abraham.

Remember when the Pharisees argued with John the Baptist? John made it clear that bloodline doesn't matter.

MATTHEW 3

9 "Don't just say to each other, 'We're safe, for we are descendants of Abraham.' That means nothing, for I tell you, God can create children of Abraham from these very stones."

John is not referring to rocks. The "stones" to which John was referring, were the people. The Pharisees considered the people to be dumb, stone-headed sheep. But the LORD considers the sheep, though many are naive and gullible, to be His precious family.

Here is the life-changing moment when Jacob, in danger from Esau's approaching band of 400 horsemen, wrestled all night with the LORD Himself! The preincarnate Christ! The dawn was about to break, but Jacob refused to let the LORD go until He blessed him!

GENESIS 28

22 "During the night Jacob got up and took his two wives, his two servant wives, and his eleven sons and crossed the Jabbok River with them.
23 After taking them to the other side, he sent over all his possessions.
24 This left Jacob all alone in the camp, <u>and a man came and wrestled with him until the dawn began to break</u>.
25 When the man saw that he would not win the match, he touched Jacob's hip and wrenched it out of its socket.
26 Then the man said,

"Let me go, for the dawn is breaking!"

But Jacob said, "I will not let you go unless you bless me."

27 "What is your name?" the man asked.

He replied, "Jacob."

28 "Your name will no longer be Jacob," the man told him. "From now on you will be called Israel, because you have fought with God and with men and have won."

29 "Please tell me your name," Jacob said.

"Why do you want to know my name?" the man replied. Then he blessed Jacob there.

30 Jacob named the place Peniel (which means "face of God"), for he said, "I have seen God face to face, yet my life has been spared."

Jacob wasn't just praying a simple prayer like "Now I lay me down to sleep." Jacob was wrestling with the LORD for the blessing of Abraham to flow through **his** family. Jacob refused to stop wrestling until he got it! That is an importunate prayer if I ever heard one! The importunate woman of Luke Chapter 18 knocked on the judge's door and kept knocking until he finally gave her the justice she wanted. That's what we are doing. Knocking on Heaven's door for justice on earth. We won't stop until we get it!

Of course the LORD could have gotten away from Jacob if He had wanted to. That's not the point. The point is that when we are in that moment of crisis…at the precipice, we call upon the LORD and that effects the change that was needed all along. The LORD doesn't need to change. We do. And wrestling prayer of faith does it. That's when Jacob won and his name was changed to Israel. That is when the dawn breaks.

The Bible doesn't say the LORD told Jacob *His* name, as Jacob had asked. Jacob didn't need to be told that. He knew he was wrestling with God Himself! The preincarnate Christ! But the LORD gave Jacob a new name! He couldn't very well go with the name Jacob which means deceiver, could he? Jacob's new name,

Israel, literally means to wrestle with God. This is a turning point of the blessing of God extending from Abraham, Isaac, and Jacob, to the entire family of God!

Humanity is wrestling with God for that blessing. We won't stop until He blesses us with freedom and justice and peace on earth! From Brazil to Venezuela to Iran to China to Canada to America. We are all wrestling, struggling, striving with God. And somehow that wrestling will effect the change we all need. As 17 said, at the precipice, when we are shown the truth, we find the will to change. We will struggle into our rightful place of authority. That's when righteous humanity will take her place as the "Israel of God." When the dawn breaks...just like the picture of the dawn breaking I put on the cover of all my End Times books.

Did you notice what Jacob named the place where He had wrestled with God?

Peniel.

Peniel means "the face of God."

Jacob had seen the face of God, and his life was spared.

Humanity will soon see the face of God, and be spared.

What does Peniel sound like?

Pineal? As in the Pineal gland?

The "God" gland?

I think the wicked want the pineal gland because they think with that gland they can defeat God. They must think it takes away our connection with God, and makes them super-evil. Ew. These people are sick.

They miss the point of the wrestling entirely. It's not to defeat God, but to struggle with Him to birth His Kingdom on earth. To be victorious! That is why the evildoers should fear Peniel. Because each of us is struggling for this Kingdom to come, His will to be done on earth as it is in Heaven. "I will not let you go unless you bless me."

Remember, the Father longs to give us the Kingdom.

LUKE 12

32 "It is the Father's good pleasure to give us the kingdom."

But the LORD must know we want His Kingdom on earth, as much as He does! We must fight for His Kingdom to come and His will to be done on earth as it is in Heaven! None of us will leave the battlefield unscathed. Notice Jacob's condition after a long night of wrestling.

GENESIS 28

31 "The sun was rising as Jacob left Peniel, and he was limping because of the injury to his hip."

Jacob never forgot that night. Just like we won't forget this long night in the battlefield. He struggled and wrestled and fought for the blessing. But it was all worth it! The Angel of the LORD said he had to go because the dawn was about to break. Jacob couldn't see His face, and live. But the dawn broke, and Jacob DID see the LORD'S face! And He lived! Jacob...now called Israel, was victorious! If you look closely, you might see His face too.

This reminds me of the song, "Nessun Dorma," that President Trump plays at every rally. The famous ballad, in Italian, is about a princess who must marry this mysterious stranger, unless she can learn his name before the dawn breaks! Yes, I know that sounds outrageous, but that's the opera for you! The princess is pleading for everyone in her country not to sleep a wink, but to help her discover the stranger's identity before the break of dawn. And the stranger is pleading for the stars to set and the dawn to break so he can win the princesses hand in marriage. The song ends with Pavarotti blasting out "Vincero!" Which means, "At dawn, I will win!" And they live happily ever after.

Want to know the mystery to "Nessun Dorma?"

Humanity is the princess in this beautiful love song. We are awake. We are wrestling...seeking God's blessing...looking for truth...looking for His face.

And the other mystery?

Our LORD Jesus is the mysterious stranger. And we will live happily ever after.

Here are the English lyrics to this amazing song and favorite of President Trump.

NESSUN DORMA
None shall sleep, None shall sleep!
Even you, oh Princess,
In your cold room,
Watch the stars,
That tremble with love
And with hope.
But my secret is hidden within me,
My name no one shall know,
No...no...
On your mouth, I will tell it,
When the light shines.
And my kiss will dissolve the silence
that makes you mine!
No one will know his name...
Vanish, o night!
Set, stars! Set, stars!
At dawn, I will win!
I will win!
I will win!

3 JOSEPH - OMER-ICA
SAVED THE WORLD

The history of God's people has more twists and turns than any fiction novel you've ever read. One minute you think all is well and everyone's going to live happily ever after. And the next minute the enemy just can't give it a rest, and here we go again. Then along comes someone who is anointed of the LORD who saves the day. In this story, that someone is Joseph. Joseph is one of my absolute favorites in all the Word of God. Joseph always followed the LORD. No matter what grief he caught. I don't think David's brothers ever read the Bible story of Joseph because they treated David just like Joseph's brothers treated him. Rude, demeaning, disrespectful...so aggravating.

Joseph was the next to the youngest son in Jacob's family of 12 sons. Jacob had four wives...at the same time. Suffice it to say, this was a very complicated family. From the get-go the Israelites were a multi-ethnic family. So don't believe the deception that all of God's people have the same skin color or all look alike. That trick is intended to throw us off the true identity of the tribes of Israel.

Jacob told Joseph to go check on his brothers, and just as Jacob suspected, they were up to no good. The Bible does not say what the brothers were doing, but they had gone to Dothan, and when they saw Joseph coming, they plotted his murder. (Genesis 37:18) They were so jealous of Joseph because of his dreams and his multi-colored royal robe their father had given him. They knew Joseph was righteous and feared that one day he would rule over them. So what were these degenerates to do? They'd been caught red-handed! They couldn't let Joseph tell Daddy

Jacob what they'd been up to. They had to get rid of the whistle-blower. I think Hillary took a lesson from these guys! That's usually what happens when someone does an evil deed...then they try to cover it up with an even more evil deed. Sounds just like the Russia hoax!

What did they do? They grabbed Joseph and threw him in a pit. Joseph was crying from that pit to let him out, and they just ignored him. If it hadn't been for their greed, they likely would have left him in there to starve and die. (By the way, the media elite allowed Donald Trump to post on social media, and they still report on his rallies, because it is so lucrative. Good thing they're greedy too!)

There was no turning back once they had thrown Joseph into that pit. Sounds just like the cabal. They have committed heinous crimes against humanity. They have tried to cover those crimes with more crimes. They know their mafia operation is like a runaway train. It runs on crime, and they just can't stop committing crimes, no matter what. At one point the cabal created a game theory model of their options. They considered whether they should confess and repent, or let the game play out? Because they knew one day they would get caught and punished. They chose to pull out all the stops and let the game play out.

In the mercy of the LORD and in His great ultimate plan, the brothers pulled Joseph out of the pit and sold him to slave traders. Away he went, never to be seen again. Or so they thought.

If they had wanted to find Joseph, where would they begin to look? Even if they did have a repentant thought, how could they ever find the slave traders and Joseph? Slave traders didn't advertise on social media back then. And then came 20+ years of agonizing guilt. How could they have done this to their very own brother? Of course Joseph was just a half brother, so no harm done. At least Daddy didn't find out about their secret mischief in Dothan. Geez. What a tangled-web they wove. Those tissue-paper thin excuses didn't cover a shred of their guilt. And the grief they put their father through for years! They saw him crying day after day after day, and they all said NOTHING. I'll go ahead and let you in on the brothers' conversations which reveal the weight of guilt they lived with.

GENESIS 42

21 "Speaking among themselves, they said, "Clearly we are being punished because of what we did to Joseph long ago. We saw his anguish when he pleaded for his life, but we wouldn't listen. That's why we're in this trouble."

22 "Didn't I tell you not to sin against the boy?" Reuben asked. "But you wouldn't listen. And now we have to answer for his blood!"...

GENESIS 44

16 "Judah answered, "Oh, my lord, what can we say to you? How can we explain this? How can we prove our innocence? God is punishing us for our sins."

GENESIS 44

27 "And your servant my father said to us, 'You know that my wife bore me two sons. 28 When one of them was gone, I said: "Surely he has been torn to pieces." And I have not seen him since. 29 Now if you also take this one from me and harm comes to him, you will bring my gray hair down to Sheol in sorrow.'

30 So if the boy is not with us when I return to your servant, and if my father, whose life is wrapped up in the boy's life, 31 sees that the boy is not with us, he will die. Then your servants will have brought the gray hair of your servant our father down to Sheol in sorrow. 32 Indeed, your servant guaranteed the boy's safety to my father, saying, 'If I do not return him to you, I will bear the guilt before you, my father, all my life.'

33 Now please let your servant stay here as my lord's slave in place of the boy. Let him return with his brothers. 34 For how can I go back to my father without the boy? I could not bear to see the misery that would overwhelm him."

This account of Judah's confession of all the brothers' guilt before God is recorded in the historical book of Jasher.

JASHER 53

31 "God has this day found the iniquity of all thy servants, therefore has he done this thing to us this day."

The brothers' consciences tormented them day and night. They were under the fear of God's judgment for what they had done. The weight of their guilt was just too heavy. Just like these brothers, humanity has far too many secrets. The truth is bursting at the seams and can't be hidden any longer. It is time for the revelation of the secrets. Just imagine the secrets the cabal is trying desperately to keep from being exposed. It's more weight than anyone can carry.

But enough about these sorry excuses for brothers! Let's follow Joseph to his destiny. Because this is our destiny too. Even though we have been under the power of these slave-traders for far too long, we will soon be exalted to positions of freedom and authority!

Imagine you're Joseph and you're headed who knows where. Imagine how Joseph must have felt. You can cry and complain and throw a fit, but the ones who own you will likely respond with a rod to the back. You can say this is all one big misunderstanding. That you don't deserve to be a slave. And that your father will gladly pay any price to have you back. "That's what *all* the slaves say. If that were true, then why did your brothers sell you in the first place?" Joseph's captors were criminals in the human-trafficking business. They had a business to run. So Joseph had to just keep walking. They might not have understood a word he said anyway.

Poor Joseph.

He just had to put one foot in front of the other.

Joseph was a young man of faith and what does a young man of faith do?

Walk by faith.

People all over the world are in very difficult predicaments where we are forced to walk by faith. So many choices are outside our control. We are born into debt slavery to the cabal. We are born into a matrix of lies and control constructs that we have no control over. We can kick and scream, and say we don't deserve this, but our masters just laugh at us, as if to say, "What are you going to do about it? Your father is not coming to rescue you." Ouch.

When Joseph arrived in this foreign land called Egypt, he was purchased as if he were a rug or a cooking pot. He was expected to do whatever he was told, whenever he was told to do it. Forget freedom. That was a thing of the past. As if that wasn't bad enough, when he refused to do evil, Joseph was lied about and thrown into prison. Forget having rights too.

Again with the familiarity. People all over the world have stood up to these tyrants and found themselves UNpopular, UNfriended, UNemployed, UNfree, or UNalive! That is the UN for you.

The story of Joseph is the story of humanity.

Enslaved.

Persecuted.

Imprisoned.

Of course at this point no one would blame Joseph if he threw up his hands and said I'm just going to have to do what I have to do to survive in this hard cruel world.

But not Joseph.

That's not Joseph's nature.

Even in prison, Joseph walked by faith and proved his character in a very difficult situation. The cream rose to the top. The chief prison guard made Joseph an overseer in the prison because Joseph was quite extraordinary. And I would also add that faithful humanity is quite extraordinary. The LORD was very proud of Joseph, and saw his faithfulness. And He's very proud of you, as you walk by faith in the middle of very difficult situations. No doubt the successes you have achieved have been because of your exemplary character and work ethic, even though the cabal tried hard to hold you down.

I'd love to tell you every detail about how Joseph rose to power in Egypt but suffice it to say the LORD gave him extraordinary gifts. Specifically, Joseph had the gift of interpreting dreams. That's always seemed like such a strange gift. No matter what your gift is, the LORD has given you exactly what you need to benefit those around you and all of humanity. It turns out, Pharaoh's cup-bearer experienced Joseph's amazing gift of dream interpretation. Pharaoh had likely gotten a bad tummy-ache. So he tossed both his chief baker and his cup-bearer into the prison where Joseph had been put in charge. It just so happened that both the chief baker and the cup-bearer had startling dreams. And it just so happened that they both told Joseph their dreams. And it just so happened that Joseph interpreted both dreams for them. Just tell me the LORD was not at work. No doubt He was setting the wheels in motion for Joseph's deliverance. Just like the dream interpretations, the chief baker was executed and the cup-bearer was freed. The cup-bearer promised to help Joseph get out of that hell-hole. But it "slipped his mind" somehow. When it served his own benefit, the cup-bearer told the king about Joseph.

We tend to blame the cup-bearer as being such a thankless weasel, letting poor Joseph rot in prison, after Joseph had helped him. But don't forget, a Pharaoh is not one for small talk with the underlings. The Pharaoh had no desire to hear of a prisoner when it had no benefit for him. So why would the cup-bearer risk his lovely neck by bringing it up? To be fair, it would likely be best told at just the right time, and that time came along. This is what happened.

Pharaoh had a dream. This was not just any dream. This dream caused him great distress.

Most dreams we forget before coffee, but not this dream. This dream nagged on his heart and his mind and he could not let it go. So he called all the wise men. But none of them could tell him the interpretation of the dream. The king was not happy. Nobody's happy when the king is not happy. So the cup-bearer raised his hand. The Pharaoh wanted someone who could interpret a dream, and the cup-bearer knew just the man he was looking for! So just that quick, Joseph was summoned from prison, bathed, and there he stood before Pharaoh. Always remember when the timing is right, the LORD is well able to deliver you from any suffering. And He will only allow the suffering for what is necessary to fulfill His perfect plans. That was a tough pill for Joseph to swallow. And for us too.

As you read the story, you'll see that Joseph did the very same thing that Daniel did. Joseph did not take the honor to himself for interpreting the dream, just like Daniel did not take the honor to himself for interpreting Nebuchadnezzar's dream.

GENESIS 41

16 "It is beyond my power to do this," Joseph replied. "But God can tell you what it means and set you at ease."

This is one more reason I admire Joseph. Pharaoh considered himself a god. Joseph was telling Pharaoh he was not. "I cannot interpret the dream but the LORD in heaven can enable me to interpret the dream." Joseph is quite impressive. When Joseph told the king the dream and the interpretation, Pharaoh was impressed too. He made Joseph manager of all the grain in Egypt.

The reason we still talk about the interpretation of Pharaoh's dream is because the LORD was foretelling a coming famine and the salvation of humanity. The LORD is able to reveal mysteries to those in authority, and cause them unease until they follow His will...even if they don't know Him! The coming famine would not just be in the land of Egypt. It would extend over all the known world. A worldwide crisis. And now you know why I'm writing about this story. The LORD laid out in His Holy Word how humanity would be saved from catastrophe, and He gave us the historical account of Joseph as a road map.

Joseph managed the storehouses of grain so well, the LORD used him to save the entire known world from starvation. The interpretation of Pharaoh's dream was that there would be seven years of plenty, when Joseph would store away grain for the coming seven years of famine. The Book of Jasher tells how others stored grain, but when the famine came, the grain was ruined because it was not stored properly. What a blessing to have someone trustworthy and wise like Joseph to manage this very important task! What a blessing that the LORD revealed this dream to the Pharaoh, and gave the interpretation to Joseph! That reminds me of how President Trump and the military have wisely prepared every move and countermove in this Great Battle, down to each precise detail!

Trust the plan!

When the seven years of famine arrived, people came from all over the world to buy grain. We read how even Joseph's father and his brothers and their families were in a desperate plight in Canaan, and were forced to go get grain from Egypt. Do you see it? Do you see the fulfillment in our day? All the world is in desperate need of being rescued from the New World Order!

Venezuela, Brazil, Iran, Mexico, Cuba, China, the African nations, the European nations, Canada...and even America. The NWO cabal is trying desperately to bring down America, because then the entire world would fall.

But America...or rather, Omer-ica, has a very special role. Actually, it has a very special **destiny** to rescue the world, just like Joseph had. The New World Order tried to make us doubt our destiny. They tried to make us believe we were under God's judgment. But that is not true. **They** are under God's judgment! We have been pushed down for far too long, and now we are rising.

They even hid the meaning of our very name from us. Our name did not come from some little-known explorer, Amerigo Vespucci. Our name comes from the "omer." Omer means grain in God's Word. We are the amber waves of grain that will save the whole world, just like Joseph did 3,800 years ago. Welcome to your destiny, Omer-ica! Thanks to President Trump, we are remembering our special role as the Omer Jubilee bundle of grain, and we will fulfill God's purpose for us. That's why nothing can stop what is coming. This is God's plan.

Our Presidential Seal has the symbols of the tribe of Manasseh...the olive branch and the arrows. Manasseh was one of Joseph's sons, who was adopted by Jacob. Manasseh received a great blessing to become a Great Nation. No doubt that has come true.

So let's see how Joseph saved his brothers, just like he had dreamed as a youth about his eleven brothers' bundles of grain bowing down to his bundle of grain. And let's see how we will save our brothers - the scattered tribes of Israel - those who love God and righteousness all over the world.

Yes, of course, the entire world went to Egypt to get grain. And that includes Joseph's brothers. This historical account has so many twists and turns, you've just got to read Exodus Chapter

5 for yourself or listen to it on *Biblegateway.com* or on the *YouVersion Bible App.*

Imagine Egypt 2,500 years ago - the hub of world commerce and wealth. And imagine Joseph dressed in the royal Egyptian garb as second in command of all of Egypt. He was overseeing the grain distribution and who did he spot? His brothers! It had been about 20 years since he had last seen them, but he could still recognize them, even if they couldn't recognize him! What would Joseph do? He could send them straight to prison. He could have his revenge on them and throw away the key, and that would be the end of that. Just like they did to him! This was just the moment he had been waiting for...the moment he could get vengeance upon his brothers for selling him into slavery. Who would blame him? Nobody. They deserved it.

But Joseph didn't do that.

Joseph had long ago realized the LORD had a much bigger plan than he or his brothers could ever have imagined, in bringing him to Egypt. He had never returned to Canaan, which surely he could have done. But that would have opened up a lot of questions that the brothers were probably not ready to answer. No. I think Joseph realized that one day his brothers would come to Egypt, and he would be able to test them to see if they had changed.

And test them, he did! This is where the Academy Award acting began. Joseph didn't tell them who he was! Joseph used his disguise to see if his brothers had changed. First, Joseph accused his brothers of being spies. He scared them half to death...which they deserved. He put them in prison for three days. He then brought them before his judgment seat, and asked them all the questions he'd been longing to know...if Benjamin was alive...if their father was alive...to which they answered yes. After he finished grilling them, he ruled that one of the brothers must stay in prison until they returned to Egypt with their younger brother! Oh dear, no! Of all the things this Egyptian ruler could ask them to do, that would be the worst! They knew their father would never allow Benjamin to come to Egypt. They had watched their father day after day after day weeping and brokenhearted for the loss of Joseph. He would never risk losing Benjamin.

What were they going to do to save their families? Their crime and cover-up hung over the family like the sword of Damocles, risking their very existence. After all these years they still couldn't find a way to confess their crime of selling Joseph into slavery. How could they confess? It would just add grief upon their father's grief to know what incorrigible, despicable excuses for humans he had raised. And they couldn't begin to know where Joseph had been taken, so what good would it do? The brothers kept this secret buried, as they were tormented daily under the weight of their guilt.

Joseph heard them talking among themselves, saying that God was punishing them for the evil they had done to Joseph.

GENESIS 42

21 "Speaking among themselves, they said, "Clearly we are being punished because of what we did to Joseph long ago. We saw his anguish when he pleaded for his life, but we wouldn't listen. That's why we're in this trouble."

22 "Didn't I tell you not to sin against the boy?" Reuben asked. "But you wouldn't listen. And now we have to answer for his blood!

23 Of course, they didn't know that Joseph understood them, for he had been speaking to them through an interpreter.

24 Now he turned away from them and began to weep. When he regained his composure, he spoke to them again."

Having no other choice, off they went back to Canaan. They left Simeon behind. When they got home they told their father,

Jacob, what happened with the ruler in Egypt. And when they said they had to return to Egypt with Benjamin, Jacob flatly refused. They knew if they didn't have Benjamin with them they would never get another kernel of grain...or Simeon! Finally, when the grain was almost gone, and there was no other option, Jacob finally allowed them to take Benjamin to Egypt for grain. It doesn't seem they were worried about Simeon rotting in prison the entire time. They all swore on their lives that they would not let one hair fall from Benjamin's head. I'm sure after all they had witnessed they would've rather experienced anything, than to see their father grieve Benjamin's death too.

But here's the part I want you to see. This is the part I want you to meditate on. This is the part that I can't tell you in its complete fulfillment. Because I believe the LORD wants to tell you Himself. Imagine this. Joseph sees his brothers, his family whom he loves, including his brother Benjamin. Can you imagine? He hasn't seen Benjamin in years. Yes, he's been successful. Yes, he has a wife and two wonderful sons. But these are his brothers. Good or bad...they are his family. And he was worried sick about how they were treating Benjamin. To see Benjamin's face and know he was alive and well, was joy and relief beyond words. Joseph literally had to leave the room to weep and compose himself.

So Joseph springs for the most elaborate banquet any of them had ever seen. Like my mom from West Tennessee says, "They put the big pot in the little one." I have no idea what that saying means...but it's a big blowout where you pull out all the stops. Joseph seated them according to their ages and they began to wonder how the ruler of Egypt would know any of that.

So Joseph put his plan into action. This was all a test to see if his brothers had changed. It is interesting the LORD had Joseph use his very special goblet for this test. It was not just an ordinary goblet like most of us thought. This very special goblet could help Joseph "tell the future." What in the world?!

Witchcraft?

No.

This goblet was a tool that somehow showed the God-ordained paths of the stars.

Remember the dream Joseph had as a youth, about the stars and the sun and the moon bowing down to him? Joseph knew all about the Mazzaroth. The Mazzaroth is the heavenly stars that make up the constellations. He knew:

GENESIS 1

14 "Then God said, "Let there be lights in the sky. These lights will separate the days from the nights. <u>They will be used for signs to show when special meetings begin</u> and to show the days and years."

The LORD put the sun, moon, and stars in the heavens for more reasons than just our calendar. Or just because they are pretty and twinkly! The LORD put them there as a heavenly clock. For example, I believe Joseph was instrumental in building and laying out the pyramids to match the constellation Orion. Truly remarkable. And intentional. The names of the stars that make up Orion describe Christ returning as the Champion to defeat the evildoers. (See the Biblical astronomy playlist on *FreedomForce.LIVE.*)

PSALM 147

4 "He counts the stars and <u>calls them all by name</u>."

PSALM 19

1 "The heavens proclaim the glory of God.
The skies display his craftsmanship.

> *2 Day after day they continue to speak;*
> *night after night they make him known.*
> *3 They speak without a sound or word;*
> *their voice is never heard."*

Clearly the LORD is saying He is speaking a message to us through the sun, moon, and stars. But most don't know how to read His messages. The enemy has hijacked the sun, moon, and stars through horoscopes, etc. But Joseph knew how to read the signs in the heavens and the <u>paths of the wandering stars</u>. This important information has been hidden from us in our day. But it is plain to see with the naked eye, that the wandering stars perform loops in the heavens. Every agrarian society has known about the wandering stars.

I think Joseph filled the great library of Egypt with this information about how to read those beautiful signs in the heavens and how to interpret them. I believe that's why they burned down the library in Egypt so we wouldn't have that information. Check the book *"The Gospel in the Stars,"* which tells the names of the stars that make up each constellation, along with each constellation's Biblical meaning. You can also following the paths of the wandering stars on the *Stellarium.org* online planetarium app. They are both very interesting and helpful.

This information is how the wise men knew about the Bethlehem Star indicating when and where the LORD Jesus, the King of the world, would be born.

And the signs in the constellations also prove this is the Battle of Armageddon to destroy the NWO Beast, because the LORD gave us the Sign of the Son of Man delineated in Revelation Chapter 12:1-2. That sign, also known as "the Woman in Labor," mentioned 18 times in the Old Testament, appeared September 23, 2017 and proves beyond a shadow of a doubt that this is the day we are being set free from our enemies.

Here is an example of just one of the circuits/loops that is happening over our heads day after day after day. This is the loop Jupiter made in Virgo's "womb" representing the labor pains, just before the Revelation 12:1-2 "Sign of the Son of Man" was completed.

REVELATION 12

1 "And then a great wonder appeared in heaven: There was a woman who was clothed with the sun, and the moon was under her feet. She had a crown of twelve stars *on her head.*

2 She was pregnant and cried out with pain because she was about to give birth."

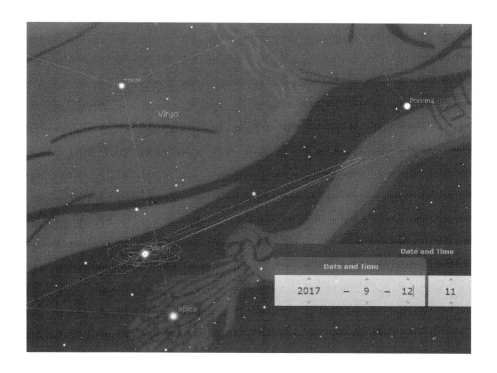

The modern Church scared us away from this information, because their cabal handlers didn't want us to decode the Book of Revelation. Thankfully, we no longer listen to them. The point for this story is that Joseph had a goblet that somehow helped him to track the circuits/loops of those wandering stars. And *that* is the goblet that was put into Benjamin's bag. Let's think about it. Joseph likely had a roomful of those goblets. But the story draws our attention to this very special goblet, that supposedly Benjamin would have wanted to steal, and Joseph would send his palace manager to retrieve. To be honest, I sure would like to have one of these goblets, if it would help me to better understand the paths God ordained for the stars!

Here is a very interesting dialogue between Joseph and Benjamin from the Book of Jasher. (If you are not familiar with Jasher, I highly recommend it. We were encouraged in Joshua 10:13 and 2nd Samuel 1:18 to read it, but most haven't. Jasher is terrific - never contradicts the Bible - it only adds more detail.)

JASHER 53

14 "And Benjamin went up before Joseph and sat upon the throne, and the men beheld the acts of Joseph, and they were astonished at them; and the men ate and drank at that time with Joseph, and he then gave presents unto them, and Joseph gave one gift unto Benjamin, and Manasseh and Ephraim saw the acts of their father, and they also gave presents unto him, and Osnath gave him one present, and they were five presents in the hand of Benjamin.

15 And Joseph brought them out wine to drink, and they would not drink, and they said, From the day on which Joseph was lost we have not drunk wine, nor eaten any delicacies.

16 And Joseph swore unto them, and he pressed them hard, and they drank plentifully with him on that day, and Joseph afterward turned to his brother Benjamin to speak with him, and Benjamin was still sitting upon the throne before Joseph.

17 And Joseph said unto him, Hast thou begotten any children? and he said, Thy servant has ten sons, and these are their names, Bela, Becher, Ashbal, Gera, Naaman, Achi, Rosh, Mupim, Chupim, and Ord, and I called their names after my brother whom I have not seen.

18 And he ordered them to bring before him his map of the stars, whereby Joseph knew all the times, and Joseph said unto Benjamin, I have heard that the Hebrews are acquainted with all wisdom, dost thou know anything of this?

19 And Benjamin said, Thy servant is knowing also in all the wisdom which my father taught me, and Joseph said unto Benjamin, Look now at this instrument and understand where thy brother Joseph is in Egypt, who you said went down to Egypt.

20 **And Benjamin beheld that** _**instrument with the map of the stars of heaven**_**, and he was wise and looked therein to know where his brother was, and Benjamin divided the whole land of Egypt into four divisions, and he found that he who was sitting upon the throne before him was his brother Joseph, and Benjamin wondered greatly, and when Joseph saw that his brother Benjamin was so much astonished, he said unto Benjamin, What hast thou seen, and why art thou astonished?**

21 **And Benjamin said unto Joseph, I can see by this that Joseph my brother sitteth here with me upon the throne, and Joseph said unto him, I am Joseph thy brother, reveal not this thing unto thy brethren; behold I will send thee with them when they go away, and I will command them** to be brought back again into the city, and I will take thee away from them.

22 And if they dare their lives and fight for thee, then shall I know that they have repented of what they did unto me, and I will make myself known to them, and if they forsake thee when I take thee, then shalt thou remain with me, and I will wrangle with them, and they shall go away, and I will not become known to them.

23 At that time Joseph commanded his officer to fill their sacks

with food, and to put each man's money into his sack, and to put the cup in the sack of Benjamin, and to give them provision for the road, and they did so unto them.

24 And on the next day the men rose up early in the morning, and they loaded their asses with their corn, and they went forth with Benjamin, and they went to the land of Canaan with their brother Benjamin."

Did you notice in verse 20 that Benjamin held the "instrument" along with the map of the stars of the heavens? I think that "instrument" was the goblet. When Benjamin looked in the goblet, he was likely able to see a loop that helped him realize this ruler sitting next to him was his very own brother, Joseph!

The entire Book of Jasher is wonderful and helps fill in so many missing blanks. But I share this account with you because clearly reading the "signs in the heavens," as the LORD put it, was common knowledge for Joseph and Benjamin. Somehow this goblet had a way to identify the loops/ciruits of the wandering stars and aid in determining their meanings. That is why the LORD put the sun, moon, and stars there for signs for us, to begin with.

This is not horoscopes.

This is not witchcraft.

This is not demonic divination.

This is Biblical astronomy.

It must be pretty important, because the cabal wants to frighten us away from discovering it!

Joseph and Benjamin set their plan into motion, and the brothers headed home with this mysterious goblet in Benjamin's sack. Right on cue, Joseph's assistants stopped them, demanding they open their sacks and return their master's goblet.

GENESIS 42

9 "If you find his cup with any one of us, let that man die. And all the rest of us, my lord, will be your slaves."

10 "That's fair," the man replied. "But only the one who stole the cup will be my slave. The rest of you may go free."

11 They all quickly took their sacks from the backs of their donkeys and opened them. 12 The palace manager searched the brothers' sacks, from the oldest to the youngest. And the cup was found in Benjamin's sack! 13 When the brothers saw this, they tore their clothing in despair. Then they loaded their donkeys again and returned to the city."

Genesis 44 says the brothers were in despair. The Book of Jasher tells that the brothers beat poor Benjamin all the way back to Egypt. It doesn't seem to me like they had changed much.

JASHER 53

*27 "And they hastened and each man brought down his sack from his ass, and they looked in their bags and the cup was found in Benjamin's bag, and they all tore their garments and they returned to the city, and they **smote Benjamin in the road, continually smiting him until he came into the city**, and they stood before Joseph."*

Bottom line: Joseph wanted to know if the brothers would protect Benjamin or if they would toss him out with the trash as they had done to him. He needed to know without a shadow of a doubt if they had changed. And this test did it. Here's the account:

GENESIS 42

14 "Joseph was still in his palace when Judah and his brothers arrived, and they fell to the ground before him. 15 "What have you done?" Joseph demanded. "Don't you know that a man like me can predict the future?"

16 Judah answered, "Oh, my lord, what can we say to you? How can we explain this? How can we prove our innocence? God is punishing us for our sins. My lord, we have all returned to be your slaves—all of us, not just our brother who had your cup in his sack."

17 "No," Joseph said. "I would never do such a thing! Only the man who stole the cup will be my slave. The rest of you may go back to your father in peace."

18 Then Judah stepped forward and said, "Please, my lord, let your servant say just one word to you. Please, do not be angry with me, even though you are as powerful as Pharaoh himself.

19 "My lord, previously you asked us, your servants, 'Do you have a father or a brother?' 20 And we responded, 'Yes, my lord, we have a father who is an old man, and his youngest son is a child of his old age. His full brother is dead, and he alone is left of his mother's children, and his father loves him very much.'

21 "And you said to us, 'Bring him here so I can see him with my own eyes.' 22 But we said to you, 'My lord, the boy cannot leave his father, for his father would die.' 23 But you told us, 'Unless your youngest brother comes with you, you will never see my face again.'

24 "So we returned to your servant, our father, and told him what you had said. 25 Later, when he said, 'Go back again and buy us more food,' 26 we replied, 'We can't go unless you let our youngest brother go with us. We'll never get to see the man's face unless our youngest brother is with us.'

27 "Then my father said to us, 'As you know, my wife had two sons,

28 and one of them went away and never returned. Doubtless he was torn to pieces by some wild animal. I have never seen him since.

29 Now if you take his brother away from me, and any harm comes to him, you will send this grieving, white-haired man to his grave.'

30 "And now, my lord, I cannot go back to my father without the boy. Our father's life is bound up in the boy's life.

31 If he sees that the boy is not with us, our father will die. We, your servants, will indeed be responsible for sending that grieving, white-haired man to his grave.

32 My lord, I guaranteed to my father that I would take care of the boy. I told him, 'If I don't bring him back to you, I will bear the blame forever.'

33 "So please, my lord, let me stay here as a slave instead of the boy, and let the boy return with his brothers.

34 For how can I return to my father if the boy is not with me? I couldn't bear to see the anguish this would cause my father!""

That was more than Joseph could take. His brothers HAD changed. Judah would rather be a slave than to see his father in anguish. Joseph sent all the assistants out of the room and he looked at his brothers. He removed his Egyptian wig. He smeared off his Egyptian makeup and said,

"It's me! I'm your brother, Joseph!"
Joseph's brothers were in complete and utter shock.
Speechless.
How could this man with such power, be their little brother, Joseph?
They were still in great fear because they knew whoever this was had power over them to end their lives.
But if this man with such power really was Joseph, then everything would change.
There was hope.
Of course, Joseph loved them and forgave them.
Joseph's brother had hard hearts...but Joseph didn't.
Their hearts had become even harder because they had never confessed their sin and received forgiveness, year after year after year.

But Joseph's tears and wailing, that were literally heard throughout Egypt, helped the brothers not to be afraid, but to rejoice that their family was back together again. They began to believe they would have a very bright future with everything they needed in Egypt. They went from the most complete sorrow and despair to the heights of joy and elation in moments! It's a wonder they didn't all have heart attacks!

That shocking transformation will happen for humanity. We are all in this epic struggle with so many sorrows and struggles, but in a moment, that will all change to complete, unbounded joy!

This is the part I want you to think about.

Joseph was there all along...watching them.

Their brother!

He was right there.

And they didn't even know it.

Think about that.

Seriously.

Put the book down.

And think about that.

The brothers were safe, and they didn't even know it. The days of waiting for restoration were over. Joseph's days of separation from his father and his family were over. Those days of restoration will be here for all of us soon.

We will understand more of God's perfect eternal plan, and our destiny in Omer-ica and as Patriots worldwide to help set the world free. And there will be tears of joy and wailing that all the world will hear.

This is Biblical.

4 MOSES - THE RED WAVE

After Joseph and the Pharaoh died, unfortunately the new Pharaoh forgot all about how Joseph had saved everyone's life. The Egyptians became jealous and afraid of the Hebrews. Little by little the Hebrews began to lose the privileges they had enjoyed. Little by little they began to lose their rights. Eventually they were taxed and worked and worked and taxed until the living conditions became unbearable. This doesn't sound familiar AT ALL!! The Egyptians began to force the Israelites to do their hard labor for them and the new Pharaoh even commanded the Israelites to throw their babies into the Nile River! Outrageous! But no more outrageous than the despicable abortion legislation still in America. Tyrants will be tyrants whether it is today or thousands of years ago.

But God was going to use Moses to deliver them from that brutal tyranny. The story of our deliverance is happening before our very eyes! The LORD has sent us our very own Moses. His name is Donald J. Trump! President Trump meant it when he said he was 'The Chosen One." He was chosen to lead humanity out of bondage. This plan started long, long ago.

You might not remember this, but Moses actually grew up in Pharaoh's palace. When Pharaoh ordered the Hebrew parents to throw their babies into the Nile, Moses' parents made him a little boat and put him in it, and his sister Miriam watched over him. Technically, they were obeying the Pharaoh. The princess discovered the little boat and took Moses to be her own son and raised him in the palace. No one but the LORD could write this story! And to top it off, the princess actually paid Moses's mother to nurse Moses until he was weaned! How remarkable is that?! God had a plan then and God has a plan now, and I don't want you to miss it! Yes Moses was an Israelite. But by growing up in the palace, he was also royalty.

I've just got to tell you that our wonderful President is true royalty. See my *FreedomForce.LIVE* playlist called *Donald Trump* and you will learn about President Trump being from both lines of the tribe of Judah. Donald J. Trump has royal blood from the line of Judah! You literally cannot make this up! President Trump has for all these years pretended to be one of 'them.' He earned their trust. He learned their secrets. He fooled them into thinking he was just like them! A wealthy, braggadocious businessman. But like Moses, Donald Trump was a man of the commoners, spending time with construction workers and tradesmen. When all along he was waiting for his opportunity to bring down these plagues on the New World Order Pharaoh! Hahahahahaha!

I think Moses had an anger management issue. While defending a Hebrew slave, Moses killed an Egyptian. Not saying the Egyptian didn't deserve it. But that was likely NOT the best way to free the Israelites from their Egyptian oppressors. So Moses fled Egypt and his royal life and went to Midian and became a shepherd. He learned how to survive in the wild, to prepare for all those years guiding the Israelites in the wilderness. Donald J. Trump hasn't done that! He has lived a large, opulent, jet-set lifestyle. He learned how to survive in the wild among New York City and Wall Street tycoons! That's an entirely different kind of wildlife. All his life, Donald J. Trump was the "golden boy." What an amazing cover! He fooled everybody! And then he came down the golden escalator and everything changed. The "golden boy" was attacked by the powers that be from that moment until this one.

Just like when Moses returned to Egypt and demanded that Pharaoh let the people go, President Trump went to Washington DC and began exposing the mafia cabal and demanded they let us go! Oh they were so mad! He's been telling us all their secrets and bringing down plagues of truth on their entire system they had built up for years. President Trump has broken the matrix of lies that held us in bondage, much like Moses broke down the Egyptians with the 10 plagues!

With one plague after another after another after another, the entire NWO system is breaking down!

No. We don't have frogs all throughout the palace. But we do have an army of frogs all throughout the internet! And we are driving them crazy!

No. The water has not turned to blood literally. But their bloody satanic rituals have certainly been exposed.

They have tried desperately to shoo away our social media posts like flies, but they can't!

Like the plague on the livestock, we've seen worldwide financial devastation. The cabal is panicking and running money laundering scams all over the place, because their assets are being seized. Since December 2017, 2,015 pages of their assets have accumulated that have been seized. They can't stop Trump!

(See www.Treasury.gov/OFAC/downloads/sdnlist.pdf)

And where will all those assets go? God's Word promises the wealth of the wicked is stored up for the righteous! So those assets will go back to the people they were stolen from! That's us! Worldwide!

What about the plague of boils? Ewwww. Sadly, many have suffered from the terrible effects of the jab, but the most heinous plague of boils is on those who participated in the disgusting and demonic practice of ingesting adrenochrome.

And the hailstones? Hailstones, which likely represent the pummeling of truth, are exposing their crimes for all to see. These plagues are devastation on the New World Order.

All these plagues in Moses' day came on the Egyptians, but God's people living in Goshen were spared. I'm sure the Egyptians forced the Hebrew slaves to clean up after all the plagues, but at least their homes were safe. As we have trusted the plan and asked the LORD to guide us though these "plagues," we have bypassed much of the misery others have suffered. But few have been left unscathed from the loss of loved ones, loss of business, and loss of relationships.

And just like the Egyptians back in Moses' day, the NWO minions are plagued, but they refuse to set the people free from their servitude. They refuse to take the consequences for all the harm they have done. They will stubbornly fight back until the prison bars slam shut.

Day after day, the Israelites complained to Moses because he was taking too long to set them free! They didn't want plagues that required them to work even harder! Moses tried to explain to them that all of this was necessary for them to be set free. He tried to encourage them to "trust the plan." Some got it. Some didn't. I'm sure Moses shrugged his shoulders and shook his head. "Do you want to be free or not?" Sounds familiar.

ACTS 14

22 *"We must go through many hardships to enter the kingdom of God," they said.*

MATTHEW 11 NKJV

12 *"And from the days of John the Baptist until now the kingdom of heaven suffers violence, and the violent take it by force."*

We are suffering many hardships to enter the kingdom of Christ on earth. But Patriots are "taking the kingdom by force." That's why we have the name "The Freedom Force Battalion." We are not playing tiddlywinks. This is war!

Now to one of the last plagues. Remember the plague of darkness? This plague reminds me of the 17 board.

"Ten days. Darkness." (post 88)

During the plagues on Egypt, the darkness only affected the Egyptians. In Goshen there was light.

How cool is that? So maybe the "Ten days. Darkness" will only affect the cabal. Either way, we will trust the plan.

Lastly, the tenth plague set the Israelites free. The firstborn of every Egyptian died, whose doorpost did not have blood from the Passover lamb. This blood represents the forgiveness that is found in Christ. Those who reject the forgiveness of God, don't get any. Before you start to think God was being harsh, remember the Egyptians murdered and enslaved the Israelites. They murdered innocent Israelite children. The Egyptians were not innocent. And neither is the cabal.

The white hats have it all.

They have every text message.

Every email.

Every financial transaction.

Every corrupt judicial ruling.

Every crime committed.

Only the guilty will be punished. The innocent will go free. This is what is promised in God's Holy Word. This is what we saw in the time of Moses, and this is what we will see very soon in our day. "This is Biblical" is on the 17 board nine times. Seventeen is not being dramatic.

We must be strong and courageous to enter into freedom. We must be unwavering in our call for justice. We must have nerves of steel and fortitude like iron to bring all the criminals to justice. They must pay for their crimes against humanity.

Treason deserves the death penalty.

We cannot wimp out.

We cannot falter.

We cannot risk these crimes against humanity ever happening again.

Their mortal wound was healed after World War II.

But Not. This. Time.

This time, the AntiChrist cabal will be cast into the abyss.

On the morning after Passover, when there was great mourning throughout Egypt, on that very day, the Israelites packed up and walked out.

With their children,

with their old,

with their sheep,

with their donkeys,

with whatever they could carry, plus more that the Egyptians begged them to take, like their silver and gold.

The Egyptians begged them to go.

The Israelites walked and walked and walked and they kept on walking. They were following Moses, who was following an amazing cloud which was the very Presence of the LORD. Always remember that. The LORD is at the head of this column of the army of digital soldiers. He is leading us out of this bondage, just as He led our Israelite ancestors 3,400 years ago. He will lead us to victory and to the Promised Land flowing with milk and honey.

We are going to enjoy 1,000 years of peace on earth. That promise of the LORD is tucked into every Bible story. He told us through the Old Testament prophets. He told us in the Book of the Revelation and Daniel and the other prophecy books. This is His promise. He has been leading all of humanity to freedom for millennia. His promises will not fail, whether we understand

His promises or not!

But, of course, the cabal won't ever give up. Remember, they are not fighting with human strength. They are fighting with evil, satanic power. These demons don't know anything about giving up. They will fight until they are literally cast into the abyss and the door is slammed shut. After all the Egyptians had been through with the plagues, Pharaoh changed his mind! He gathered his army and chased after the Israelites to haul them back to do all the work! Unbelievable! Tyrants gotta tyrant.

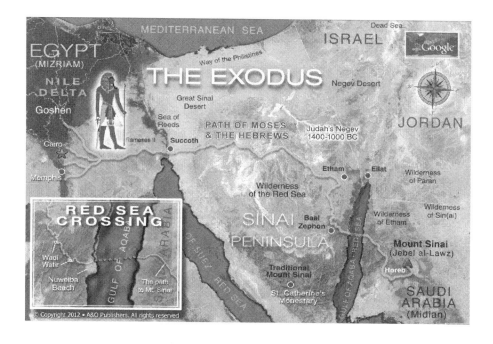

The Israelites walked all the way to the Red Sea. This was where the LORD in the cloud led them. They had no idea what to do next but they had no choice but to trust the plan. Then the Israelites looked back and saw the Egyptians hot on their heels! What were they going to do? There was nowhere to run. Nowhere to hide a couple million people! It was hopeless. But... the LORD had led them to this precipice...on purpose. They were between a rock and a hard spot. Hemmed in by mountains on both sides and the Red Sea in front of them. And the Egyptian army was closing in behind them. That's a precipice if I ever heard of one. Humanity must go to the precipice, just like our Israelite forefathers did. Collective humanity must see God's hand alone save us. We must walk across the dry seabed together, and watch as our enemies are destroyed.

God had not brought the Israelites through all those plagues and set them free, and brought them all the way to the Red Sea, just for them to turn back to slavery. The same goes for humanity in our day. Patriots in every country are rising up against these tyrants because of the Great Awakening! The LORD has brought us this far. He has planned our salvation for literally thousands of years. There is no turning back. We have no choice. Just like our Israelites' forefathers. We can be afraid when we see these NWO minions charging toward us. Or we can trust the LORD. Let's focus on those same words from Moses "Stand still and see the salvation of the LORD."

Nuweiba Beach, Egypt
Area : 28 Km²
Mountains: 500 m
www.bible.ca

That's what the Freedom Force Battalion is all about. And that's just what we're going to do. We're going to stand still and we're going to see the salvation of the LORD. That is what President Trump says at every rally.

We will not bend.

We will not break.

We will never give in.

We will never give up.

We will never ever back down.

We will make America great again.

And I take that to mean every country will be great again.

Just look at what God did. There were no other options except for the salvation of the LORD. There was nothing else to do except watch and see a miracle from the hand of the Living God. The LORD literally blew with the blast of his nostrils and opened the Red Sea and the ground became dry. The Israelites walked right through.

They didn't have to push the water up. God did that.

They didn't have to dry the seabed. God did that.

They simply walked through.

And the fools...the Deep State mafia cabal Egyptian fools followed them right into the Red Sea. How stupid could they be?! It reminds me of Shifty Shift and Nancy-pants and Chuckie and Biden and Soros and Fauci and Gates and Zuckerburg who fall into President Trump's and the white hats' trap time and time and time again. They are exposing themselves as the criminals they are. The Red Sea is crashing in on them! We will watch them as they are brought up on charges and exposed before the entire world in public shame. We will see how the LORD is going to do it, in His perfect timing.

One way or another, these tyrants will drown in a Red Sea moment and we will enter the Promised Land. We will enter days of freedom and health and wealth that none of us right now can imagine, just like our Israelite ancestors could not have imagined.

LORD remove from us our slave mentality.

LORD remove from us any fear.

LORD give us the strength by Your Spirit to stand and see Your great salvation.

5 MOSES - LAW AND ORDER

Remember the "The 10 Commandments" movie and the amazing scene of the LORD opening up the Red Sea and God's people walking through?! Remember all the Egyptian soldiers racing in after them with their horses and chariots, and being covered over by the Red Sea crashing down on them?! They don't make movies like they used to, do they? Imagine yourself there...one moment in a desperate predicament, afraid for your life and your family and friends...and the next moment, you and your loved ones are safely on the other side, and your enemies are:

DECIMATED!

DESTROYED!

GONE!

No wonder they told this story at every Passover and sang songs about the great way the LORD saved them! There was literally no denying it. Everyone heard what happened, even without the internet! And everyone was afraid of the God of Moses!

We are at the Red Sea, my friends. Soon we will be on the other side, and our enemies will be:

DECIMATED!

DESTROYED!

GONE!

Everyone must see it. Everyone must understand what these evildoers have done...from the poison jab intentionally causing sudden deaths, to the destruction of our border security and sovereignty, to the financial devastation, to the gender confusion, to the loss of our freedoms. Everyone must know WHO is responsible, so we can rejoice together as they are "hurled into the sea!"

Once the Israelites were safe, they sang an amazing song and it starts like this...

EXODUS 15

1b "I will sing to the LORD for

He has triumphed gloriously;

he has hurled both horse and rider into the sea!"

I'm sure it was in the Top 40 back in the day!

EXODUS 15

A Song of Deliverance

1 "Then Moses and the people of Israel

sang this song to the Lord:

"I will sing to the Lord,

for he has triumphed gloriously;

he has hurled both horse and rider into the sea.

2 The Lord is my strength and my song;

he has given me victory.

This is my God, and I will praise him—

my father's God, and I will exalt him!

3 The Lord is a warrior;

Yahweh is his name!

4 Pharaoh's chariots and army

he has hurled into the sea.

The finest of Pharaoh's officers

are drowned in the Red Sea.

5 The deep waters gushed over them;

they sank to the bottom like a stone.

6 "Your right hand, O Lord, is glorious in power.

Your right hand, O Lord, smashes the enemy.

7 In the greatness of your majesty,

you overthrow those who rise against you.

You unleash your blazing fury;

it consumes them like straw.

8 At the blast of your breath,

the waters piled up!

The surging waters stood straight like a wall;

in the heart of the sea the deep waters became hard.

9 "The enemy boasted, 'I will chase them

and catch up with them.

I will plunder them and consume them.

I will flash my sword;

my powerful hand will destroy them.'

10 But you blew with your breath,

and the sea covered them.

They sank like lead in the mighty waters.

11 "Who is like you among the gods, O Lord—

glorious in holiness, awesome in splendor,

performing great wonders?

12 You raised your right hand,

and the earth swallowed our enemies.

13 "With your unfailing love you lead

the people you have redeemed.

In your might, you guide them to your sacred home.

14 The peoples hear and tremble;

anguish grips those who live in Philistia.
15 The leaders of Edom are terrified;
the nobles of Moab tremble.
All who live in Canaan melt away;
16 terror and dread fall upon them.
The power of your arm makes them lifeless as stone
until your people pass by, O Lord,
until the people you purchased pass by.
17 You will bring them in and
plant them on your own mountain—
the place, O Lord, reserved for your own dwelling,
the sanctuary, O Lord, that your hands have established.
18 The Lord will reign forever and ever!"
19 When Pharaoh's horses, chariots, and charioteers
rushed into the sea, the Lord brought the water crashing
down on them. But the people of Israel
had walked through the middle of the sea on dry ground!
20 Then Miriam the prophet, Aaron's sister,
took a tambourine and led all the women as they played
their tambourines and danced.
21 And Miriam sang this song:
"Sing to the Lord, for he has triumphed gloriously;
he has hurled both horse and rider into the sea."

One of my favorite lines is:

8 "At the blast of your breath, the waters piled up!
The surging waters stood straight like a wall;"

Every Passover celebration includes the retelling of how the LORD saved His people in this amazingly miraculous way! We have all looked back on this one event more than any other, for courage and faith. That's what Passover is all about! The LORD is clearly able to deliver us from the hands of these evil tyrants! Never let that song leave your heart! The LORD has triumphed gloriously; he has hurled horse and rider into the sea! We will rejoice and rejoice and rejoice when our enemies are hurled into the sea! This time it will be for all of humanity, once and for all! We have been under their rule and fought to expose them for so long, it's next to impossible to imagine. But we will see that day. Just as the LORD promised in Isaiah 41:12, we will look for our enemies and not be able to find them.

Do you remember where the Israelites headed next?

The LORD in the column of cloud led them to Mount Sinai to receive the 10 Commandments. The people had never learned how to have a just and free society. They had only experienced tyranny. All they had done was menial labor from sun up to sun down.

Unfortunately, we are in a similar boat in our day. We are all taking crash courses in Civics 101, Bill of Rights 101, House of Representative Rules 101, Elections 101, Electoral College 101, and Supreme Court 101. And we're just getting started!

Poor Moses was starting from scratch. The first place to go was to Mount Sinai for a heaping helping of law and order. God gave them the 10 Commandments and rules about how to approach Him and receive forgiveness, and how to keep their society unified. They needed to know the rules and know the consequences for breaking those rules, or their society would be destroyed from within. By most accounts, around two and a half million Israelites left Egypt with Moses. But even that number could be obliterated, if they did not follow law and order.

Mount Sinai terrified the Israelites.
Lightning flashed and thunder crashed.

Everyone was warned not to touch the mountain because the holiness and justice of God had descended on the mountain. The people were terrified. Moses ascended to the top of Mount Sinai to receive the 10 Commandments from the LORD. He was gone for 40 days.

Aaron and Miriam were left in charge. Of 2.4 million people. You can imagine the people became bored and impatient waiting for Moses to return. After weeks went by they figured Moses must have died on that rocky barren wasteland. They didn't know what to do. I'm sure they were scared and uncertain what their future would be like. They didn't know how to worship the true and living God. So when Moses came down the mountain, he discovered them worshiping a golden calf! Literally worshiping Baal, just as they had seen in Egypt and had been brainwashed into believing! Can you just imagine the look on Aaron's face? These people were a hot mess! Moses took the people out of

Egypt, but it would take a lot more to take the Egypt out of the people! To establish law and order would be a tough road ahead.

The good news for us is that we already have established laws. The bad news is that those laws haven't been followed as they should. Just look at the crime rates, the border crisis, the election debacle...and the outrageous government corruption!

We are experiencing what happens to a society when the people don't know right from wrong, and when the judges don't rule right from wrong. The justice system has been turned on its head! The guilty go free and the righteous are punished! Some of the twisted, unconstitutional, and even communistic thought processes we see and hear are appalling. How in the world will we ever untangle the evil satanic knots the education system and the media have woven into the hearts and minds of the people? How will we instill the understanding of liberty and justice for all?

Soon the people will realize the heinous crimes the NWO has committed against them...likely starting with the poisonous jab...and they will be screaming for justice. When judgment falls on the cabal, that will move our society strongly in the direction of law and order. This will be a lesson humanity will not soon forget! No one will ever consider doing such evil because the consequences will be terrifying. We all MUST ascend Mount Sinai. That is the only way for us to have society set right with Law and Order, so humanity is not obliterated.

THE FEAR OF OBLITERATION *IS* THE PRECIPICE.

Most of the problems we face can be rectified rather quickly, when we have righteous judges in authority. News of serious consequences will spread quickly, and bring most into compliance. That strong justice meted out will help to bring about 1,000 years of peace on earth.

Here is what Revelation 11 says will happen when an earthquake of justice falls on the criminals at the top. The rest were terrified and repented.

REVELATION 11

13 "And at that time there was a great earthquake, and a tenth of the city fell; seven thousand people were killed in the earthquake, and the rest were terrified and gave glory to the God of heaven."

Law and Order is wonderful.

Love it.

It keeps humanity from being obliterated.

We will be able to rest safely in our beds.

We will be able to walk safely on the streets.

Everyone will know that if they do the crime, they will have to do the time.

The guilty will be punished; not the righteous.

No ifs, ands, or buts.

But...we need grace too.

We need forgiveness, and to forgive one another.

We need the Presence of God for discernment.

Here is an example of how the LORD strikes that balance. While Moses was on the mountain, the LORD told him the people were literally worshiping Baal at the base of Mount Sinai! The LORD told Moses He wanted to destroy them all on the spot! The LORD said He would make a great nation from Moses, rather than from Abraham. (The LORD said this to test Moses.) Moses pleaded for the people and for the LORD to forgive them and to work with them. But then Moses came down the mountain and saw what they were doing with his very own eyes! He was so angry he threw down and broke the 10 Commandments the LORD had just inscribed with very His own finger!

The reason I bring this up, is because there are horrific things we will see and discover over the next few years that will make us all so angry that we will want to obliterate every person remotely involved. Justice requires nerves of steel AND the discernment of Solomon. As the Habakkuk asked the LORD...

HABAKKUK 3

2b "And in your anger, remember your mercy."

The only way humanity can ascend is by the literal Presence of God. We need the spell of evil to be broken, and for the LORD to pour out His Spirit on all flesh. Then the earth will be filled with the knowledge of the LORD as the waters fill the sea.

The Israelites had a brilliant ray of hope of the Presence of God. Remember the Israelites still carried Jacob's Pillar with them, which Jacob had found on Beth El when he was running away from Esau. The LORD'S Presence was with them and He would take care of their every need. Here is an instance when the people were complaining for water, and the LORD provided through *Jacob's Pillar*, also known as the *Stone of Destiny.*

EXODUS 17

5 "The Lord said to Moses, "Walk out in front of the people. Take your staff, the one you used when you struck the water of the Nile, and call some of the elders of Israel to join you.

6 I will stand before you on the rock at Mount Sinai. Strike the rock, and water will come gushing out. Then the people will be able to drink." So Moses struck the rock as he was told, and water gushed out as the elders looked on."

The LORD stood before Moses on the rock, and when Moses struck the rock, water gushed out it!
Wow!
That must have been a sight!
The rock was only about two feet long and one foot wide!

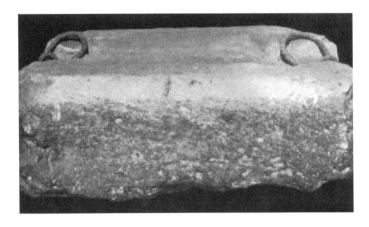

The *Stone of Destiny* also known as *Jacob's Pillar* was not attached to the ground or to a spring.

WATER LITERALLY CAME OUT OF THE ROCK!

It wasn't a thimbleful of water.

It wasn't a cupful.

The rock poured forth water for 2.4 million people!

WOW!

It was such a comfort knowing the LORD was with them and would provide their needs. They had access to an ever-flowing stream of refreshing water no matter where they went! They had the life-giving water they needed. And more importantly, as recorded in 1st Corinthians Chapter 10, that rock was Christ.

1st CORINTHIANS 10

*3 "All of them ate the same spiritual food, and all of them drank the same spiritual water. 4 For they drank from the spiritual rock that traveled with them, and **that rock was Christ.**"*

That rock was Christ.

And that, my friends, is our hope.

Our Lord Jesus with us.

To provide our every need.

To cast out the satan worshipers.

To rule His Millennial Kingdom.

To guide us, far better than law books.

The life-giving water to sustain us.

Walking and talking with us like with His disciples.

Living with us.

The Word of God, in flesh.

As John said,

JOHN 1

14 "the Word became flesh and dwelt among us and we beheld His glory!"

The LORD will be with us in this Millennial Kingdom. The LORD **Himself** will live among us as He promised in Zephaniah Chapter 3 and Obadiah Chapter 1.

ZEPHANIAH 3

17 "He is a mighty savior.
He will take delight in you with gladness.
With his love, he will calm all your fears.
He will rejoice over you with joyful songs."

OBADIAH 1

21 "The Lord Himself will be King."

All will know Him from the least to the greatest. He will continually give us the understanding and the power to have 1,000 years of peace and justice on earth. This **will** be fulfilled as promised in Amos Chapter 5.

AMOS 5

24b "a mighty flood of justice,
an endless river of righteous living."

How we could we ever have 1,000 years of justice and righteousness and peace on earth? We haven't even been able to have real peace with our neighbors, much less with all of humanity! In the same way, the disciples did not have the power to go into all the world and preach the gospel, until the LORD poured out His Spirit on them. Then and only then could they complete that monumental task of the Great Commission. Somehow, some way, the LORD will empower us to do this.

First, this ridiculous, exhausting, aggravating, cabal-fomented division and tyranny and deception and war will end. We will have righteous laws and righteous judges. And...the LORD will pour out His Spirit on ALL flesh.

That is how.
The promise of peace on earth is clear in God's Word.

HABAKKUK 2

14 "For as the waters fill the sea, the earth will be filled with an awareness of the glory of the LORD."

JOEL 2

28 "I will pour out my Spirit upon all people.
Your sons and daughters will prophesy.
Your old men will dream dreams,
and your young men will see visions.

29 In those days I will pour out my Spirit
even on servants—men and women alike."

By His Spirit poured out on humanity, we will have true lasting peace. We will have peace on earth, goodwill towards men. We've gotten a sampling of world peace under the Trump administration, and here's what the LORD promises to do:

ISAIAH 2

4 "The Lord will mediate between nations and will settle

international disputes. They will hammer their swords into plowshares and their spears into pruning hooks. Nation will no longer fight against nation, nor train for war anymore."

And this verse from Revelation 20, loaded with symbolism, will be fulfilled.

REVELATION 20

4 *"**Then I saw thrones, and the people sitting on them had been given the authority to judge.** And I saw the souls of those who had been beheaded for their testimony about Jesus and for proclaiming the word of God. They had not worshiped the beast or his statue, nor accepted his mark on their foreheads or their hands. **They all came to life again, and they reigned with Christ for a thousand years.***

5 This is the first resurrection. (The rest of the dead did not come back to life until the thousand years had ended.)

*6 Blessed and holy are those who share in the first resurrection. **For them the second death holds no power, but they will be priests of God and of Christ and will reign with him a thousand years.**"*

It appears from this verse, that in the Millennial Kingdom we will have leaders whom we can trust. And they will be given the special ability to guide us, to make righteous laws, and to appoint righteous judges and managers. It also appears that they will be given life extension. For example, imagine how we could trust Moses if he were on earth. And Daniel. And Joseph. That way, 500 years from now, people will be able connect back to this day when the Beast tyrannized the world, and fake news won't be able to deceive people about it. Much like when we read a "truth" from President Trump and he destroys the fake news!

These leaders will have proven they have the courage and the wisdom and the fortitude to guide us into these beautiful days. Beautiful days that we can hardly imagine now. Everyone will know their guidance is trustworthy. That's what this passage sounds like to me. We will see.

Isaiah Chapter 65 helps us to imagine the brilliant days ahead. The people will live as long as trees! What beautiful imagery!

ISAIAH 65

21 "In those days people will live in the houses they build and eat the fruit of their own vineyards.
22 Unlike the past, invaders will not take their houses and confiscate their vineyards.
For my people will live as long as trees,
and my chosen ones will have time

to enjoy their hard-won gains.
23 They will not work in vain,
and their children will not be doomed to misfortune.
For they are people blessed by the Lord,
and their children, too, will be blessed.
24 I will answer them before they even call to me.
While they are still talking about their needs,
I will go ahead and answer their prayers!
25 The wolf and the lamb will feed together.
The lion will eat hay like a cow.
But the snakes will eat dust.
In those days no one will be hurt
or destroyed on my holy mountain.
I, the Lord, have spoken!"

Health! Wealth! Restoration!
Law and Order...and True, Lasting Peace!
Finally.
The LORD has spoken!

6 JOSHUA - THE FALL
OF THE CABAL

You've got to love Joshua! No wonder so many parents name their son Joshua. For 40 years in the desert Joshua was Moses's faithful assistant. After the Israelites crossed the Red Sea and received the 10 Commandments, the people were supposed to go straight into the Promised Land of Canaan - the land flowing with milk and honey! Moses sent 12 spies to scope out the land. Ten of the spies came back shaking in their boots, afraid of the "giants" who lived in Canaan. But Joshua and Hur came back reporting that the land was wonderful and that they could defeat the people of Canaan! I love that positive attitude of faith!

To be honest there are far too many "Negative Nellies" in the Patriot movement! I don't know if they are trolls or just negative people, but I wish they'd give it a break and be more like Joshua and Hur! If the people of Israel had just trusted God and listened to Joshua and Hur, they could have avoided 40 years of wandering in the desert. They could've gone on into the Promised Land and avoided all that misery! But, they weren't ready to take the land! They weren't ready to be free.

That is one of the key lessons humanity **must** learn. Most have not been ready to take this freedom! Most have not been ready to live free, and still cannot find it within themselves to <u>think for themselves</u>! <u>Most still just want to be told what to think</u>. Most are so accustomed to being oppressed under the thumb of the "authorities" telling them what to do, and how to do it, and when to do it, (like a mask and a jab) they just can't grasp self-government as a free human being. They just can't say NO to their masters. That's why humanity has been wandering in this desert for millennia under these over-bearing tyrants who make agreements for **their** best interests, and not for ours! They grab up all the wealth and resources for themselves, and leave us to scrap for nickels! It's time to take the Promised Land! It's time for humanity to be free! Ready or not, we have no choice. The only other option is hell on earth under the New World Order's brutal tyranny.

Joshua knew how to think for himself and to be free. He had learned well under Moses's tutelage. Very rarely do you find a hero in God's Word without a glaring character flaw, but Joshua is one of those who always showed exemplary character and faith. He received great blessings for that faithfulness. Joshua was chosen to lead the people in the battles to take the Promised Land.

The first battle to take Canaan was for the city of Jericho. I'm sure you've heard the song "Joshua fought the battle of Jericho and the walls came tumbling down." The people of Jericho had very high walls around their city...likely to prevent anyone from stopping their atrocities. Do you know what was inside those walls? The people of Jericho were Canaanites. Canaanites as in CANNIBALS. That, my friends, is why the LORD commanded the Israelites to destroy every Canaanite man, woman, and child. I don't think most of us understood that. In the back of our minds we thought maybe the LORD was being a little harsh by destroying them all. But these people had committed themselves to demons and would do whatever the demons led them to do. That is why the Canaanites had to be eliminated completely. That is why the LORD told Joshua the people could not intermarry with them. It was not about ethnicity! It was not that the Israelites considered themselves superior to other people. The Israelites were to be a *holy* people. Holy as in filled with the *Holy* Spirit instead of filled with demonic spirits. Joshua was determined to follow the LORD'S instructions to the letter.

Joshua sent two spies into Jericho to scope it out. Word spread throughout Jericho that there were spies in the city. Just like now, there are minions on the payroll in every town, watching to protect the power structure, always eager to report suspicious patriot activity to their handlers. The soldiers immediately began searching everywhere. Joshua's spies found the perfect hiding spot! In the home of Rahab, a prostitute. The LORD directed them there for good reason...because Rahab was a woman who knew how to keep a secret, and who to tell a secret! And she knew how to get men to tell her **their** secrets! Plus, she was an accomplished liar! Quite the talent!

Here's the account from Joshua Chapter 2:

JOSHUA 2

4 "Rahab had hidden the two men, but she replied, "Yes, the men were here earlier, but I didn't know where they were from.

5 They left the town at dusk, as the gates were about to close. I don't know where they went. If you hurry, you can probably catch up with them."

6 (Actually, she had taken them up to the roof and hidden them beneath bundles of flax she had laid out.)

7 So the king's men went looking for the spies along the road leading to the shallow crossings of the Jordan River. And as soon as the king's men had left, the gate of Jericho was shut.

8 Before the spies went to sleep that night, Rahab went up on the roof to talk with them.

9 "I know the Lord has given you this land," she told them. "We are all afraid of you. Everyone in the land is living in terror.

10 For we have heard how the Lord made a dry path for you through the Red Sea when you left Egypt. And we know what you did to Sihon and Og, the two Amorite kings east of the Jordan River, whose people you completely destroyed.

11 No wonder our hearts have melted in fear! No one has the courage to fight after hearing such things. For the Lord your God is the supreme God of the heavens above and the earth below.

12 "Now swear to me by the Lord that you will be kind to me and my family since I have helped you. Give me some guarantee that

13 when Jericho is conquered, you will let me live, along with my father and mother, my brothers and sisters, and all their families."

14 "We offer our own lives as a guarantee for your safety," the men agreed. "If you don't betray us, we will keep our promise and be kind to you when the Lord gives us the land."

15 Then, since Rahab's house was built into the town wall, she let them down by a rope through the window.

16 "Escape to the hill country," she told them. "Hide there for three days from the men searching for you. Then, when they have returned, you can go on your way."

This chapter is loaded with great clues!

Did you notice Rahab hid the spies ON HER ROOF, which was part of the city walls? She had flax bundles laid out on her roof, so she had access to the roof all the time. Likely most of the Jericho walls were homes like Rahab's, with roof access. Remember that for later.

While we are at it, notice that the spies hid under bundles of flax...which are basically "Omer"...as in Omer-ica (America). America is the safest place on earth from the NWO thugs.

When the soldiers asked if she had seen the spies, Rahab batted her eyes and lied saying, *"They went that way! If you hurry maybe you can catch them."* They fell for it and hurried away! I bet she had used that trick many a time, when a wife was looking for her no-account cheating husband! That trickery earned Rahab a place in the famous Hall of Faith in Hebrews Chapter 11!

Disinformation is necessary! Rahab knew that. She was a terrific deceiver! President Trump says he will never announce his plans to our enemies. The enemies he is talking about, are the New World Order! LORD make us better liars! This is not a game. This is war. One of the reasons the criminals have run roughshod over us is because they are very skilled at lying and we are not!

How did Rahab know the king's men were looking for the spies along the road leading to the shallow crossings of the Jordan River? And that as soon as the king's men had left, the gate of Jericho was shut? Because she has womanly wiles that make foolish men tell their secrets!

Once she got that intel from the soldiers, she told the Israelite spies to *"Escape to the hill country and hide there for three days from the men searching for you. Then, when they have returned, you can go on your way."*

That intel likely saved the spies' lives. Great job Rahab!

It's kind of interesting that the LORD gives us that little tidbit about the spies hiding for **three days**. I wonder if He's telling us through symbolism (a day is a thousand years to God) that humanity would be "hiding" from these creeps for about 3,000 years after the Battle of Jericho, when we would finally be free of them! Interesting thought...because that's where we are on the history timeline!

Before the spies left, Rahab told them that everyone knew God was with the Israelites and that they would be victorious over Jericho. Everyone knew how the Israelites' God worked miracles for them that no other god could overcome. Rahab asked the spies to protect her and all her people when they destroyed Jericho. They promised they would, and she tied a red scarf of redemption on her window as a sign that she was to be protected.

Once she had secured her safety and the safety of her people, she let the spies escape out her window which was on the city wall! I'm sure she'd used that trick before too!

This was the report the spies told Joshua:

JOSHUA 2

23 *"Then the two spies came down from the hill country, crossed the Jordan River, and reported to Joshua all that had happened to them.*

24 *"The Lord has given us the whole land," they said, "for all the people in the land are terrified of us.""*

I know Joshua was so happy to hear that the people of Jericho were filled with panic Panic PANIC! The people of Jericho knew they would be defeated! No doubt the LORD had struck fear into their hearts, just like the New World Order is in panic mode. They know we're going to defeat them. It's just a matter of time.

Joshua was ready to lead the people to take the Promised Land. The most wonderful blessing was that the LORD spoke directly to him. The LORD told Joshua it was time to cross the Jordan and defeat the Canaanites. He told him to be strong and courageous. And the LORD promised to be with him and give him victory. Joshua stood on those promises. We are doing the same.

Joshua instructed the tribes of Reuben, Gad, and Manasseh to prepare for this battle and to help the people cross the Jordan River. The LORD was going to show this generation a miracle much like the Red Sea miracle, to give them courage that He was leading them and would give them victory. As always, when the people of Israel would travel, the priests would lead the way with the Ark of the Covenant. The Ark was always covered with a large curtain because the people were not allowed to look upon it. And the priests carried the Ark with poles, because they were not allowed to touch it. Looking at the Ark or touching the Ark was the same as looking upon the LORD Himself and touching Heaven...and you would go straight there! In a very similar way, we might not see the LORD, but we know He is with us, and He is guiding us step by step into the Promised Land.

The priests led the way to the Jordan River, carrying the Ark of the Covenant, and the people followed. As the priests put their feet into the river, the water stood up in a heap and the ground dried up! Just like at the Red Sea! The priests stayed with the Ark of the Covenant in the middle of the Jordan River, so all the people walked by it and knew the LORD was with them and not to be afraid. Imagine that! Walking across the Jordan River on dry ground, and seeing the Ark of the Covenant covered with a curtain – the physical manifestation of the True and Living God! The Ark was almost always kept in the Tabernacle and the people couldn't go in, but this time they were seeing the Ark holding back the river for them! That gave them so much confidence to trust the plan! That's our job in this Battle of Armageddon...to remind everyone the LORD is with us and He is leading us to victory!

When everyone got to the other side of the Jordan River, each of the 12 tribes took a stone from the river and set them up in Gilgal as a memorial to their years in the desert. Then the Israelites set up camp to prepare to take the city of Jericho. After the Battle of Armageddon is over, we will have memorials set up to remind humanity of the many years we spent under the tyranny of the New World Order. Every country will have its own memorials to remind everyone what happened, so this will never happen again!

The king of Jericho heard reports of how the people crossed the Jordan River on dry ground. The king of Jericho and all the people were paralyzed with fear! They had never seen a god that could do that! Their demon gods certainly couldn't! Word spread like wildfire. Fear spread along with it!

The Israelites camped in Gilgal which means "to roll," as in the shame of slavery had been rolled away. The LORD was removing their shame. Once these evildoers are cast out, all the shame of humanity will be rolled away forever!

JOEL 2

27 "Then you will know that I am among my people Israel, that I am the LORD your God, and there is no other. Never again will my people be disgraced."

The Israelites consecrated themselves for the battle ahead. We on the Freedom Force Battalion are doing the same. We are dedicated to seeking the LORD'S guidance through His Word and prayer, and we are dedicated to living lives that honor Him and to fight alongside Him in this Great Battle of Armageddon. Time to slough off all the bondage of slavery, and to take the Kingdom of Christ by force!

One day Joshua was near Jericho and a Man with a sword appeared to him. He said He was not friend or foe. He was the Commander of the LORD'S army. He told Joshua to remove his sandals because he was standing on holy ground. In other words, Joshua was face-to-face with the Angel of the LORD - the preincarnate Christ! The LORD was meeting with Joshua to **give** him instructions for the battle.

JOSHUA 6

2 "I have given you Jericho, its king, and all its strong warriors.

3 You and your fighting men should march around the town once a day for six days.

4 Seven priests will walk ahead of the Ark, each carrying a ram's horn. On the seventh day you are to march around the town seven times, with the priests blowing the horns.

5 When you hear the priests give one long blast on the rams' horns, have all the people shout as loud as they can. Then the walls of the town will collapse, and the people can charge straight into the town."

WOW! What an amazing battle plan! Because it wasn't a typical battle plan at all! Much like the unconventional battle we are fighting as digital soldiers on the digital battlefield. The LORD'S plan was to cause the walls of Jericho to collapse, by just marching and blowing trumpets and shouting. Think for a minute how crazy that sounds. But the people trusted the plan. And the LORD brought the walls of Jericho crashing down! So, let's trust the plan everybody!

Joshua passed along these instructions to the people. The people lined up to go on the march. Seven priests in the front with their ram's horns, and then the Ark of the Covenant of the LORD, along with some of the armed men, and then about a half mile back, the people followed. The instructions were simple. The priests would blow their trumpets, and the people would march quietly without saying a word all the way around the city, and then return to camp. That was it.

The people had been waiting for **40** years to take the Promised

Land. And that was all they did! They just walked around the city and went back to camp. That's it?! Isn't that how we feel, Patriots? We've just been walking around and around and we want to get this show on the road! We want to see all the arrests! We want heads to roll! On the second day, Joshua gave the same instructions from the LORD. March around the city without saying a word and then return to camp. The people did exactly as they were instructed, just like we have. Every day we share information just as we've been told to do, marching around the city and waiting for further instructions. Guess what they did the third day. The same thing. And the fourth. And the fifth. And the sixth day too. Not a word...just march around the city and return to camp. The Israelites might have felt ridiculous. They might have felt exasperated...that this entire march was a waste of time. I don't know if they did. They were probably still super-charged with faith, since crossing the Jordan River on dry ground, and they trusted the plan! We could take a lesson from them.

Over the past several years I've read lots of complaints about why draining the swamp is taking so long. Do you see how this is part of the strategy? The people of Jericho were freaked out by this very unusual display, as they watched from the tops of the walls of Jericho. They could not figure it out. Think about it. Most human reasoning would have been to use a battering ram to break through Jericho's walls. Most modern military commanders would have arrested the Deep State criminals long ago. And let's be honest. The likelihood of those plans blowing up in their faces would have been enormous. We have one shot at saving humanity. This operation must be done perfectly, with exact military precision. This must be done God's way. So if anyone has any complaints, take it up with the LORD!

But finally, the Israelites arrived at the seventh day. Seven is a very significant number. A number of completion. In creation, the LORD rested on the seventh day. Since Adam and Eve, humanity has been going round and round for six full millennia. We are now entering the seventh millennia. See how the recorded account of the Battle of Jericho gives us major clues, if we just look for them? No doubt this is our Day of Victory over our enemies!

On the seventh day, the people of Jericho were watching for the usual parade of Israelites around the city walls. But something different happened on the seventh day. The Israelites kept walking. They didn't go home! Then the Israelites completed two circuits around the walls of Jericho. Still without making a peep! What do you bet the people went up on their rooftops to see what was happening? The Israelites completed a third circuit around the walls, and more people went to their rooftops to watch. Then a fourth circuit, and then a fifth, and a sixth.

By this time, I bet just about everyone in Jericho was watching from a rooftop along the wall to see what was going to happen. Fear and dread were filling the minds. What in the world were the Israelites doing? The people of Jericho couldn't understand it any more than the New World Order can understand the plans of this incredible military operation.

"Nothing is happening."
If I have heard it once, I've heard it 1,000 times.
"Nothing is happening."

But then.

On the **seventh** day...

On the **seventh** circuit around the walls,

SOMETHING HAPPENED.

The priests blew a loud blast with their trumpets. That signaled for the people to start shouting. The priests kept blowing their trumpets and the people kept shouting until something happened. The walls of Jericho literally started to crumble. Between all the sound waves and all the people on top of the walls, the walls of Jericho broke completely apart and fell down flat! All the people on top of the walls fell down with it!

What a plan!

The people who were surrounding the walls, charged into the city from every side...like spokes on a wheel. The people of Jericho were utterly defenseless! Every man, woman, and child in Jericho...every Baal-worshiping cannibal...was destroyed! Except for Rahab and her people protected by the scarlet cord of redemption.

JOSHUA 6

24 "The Israelites burned the town and everything in it. Only the things made from silver, gold, bronze, or iron were kept for the treasury of the Lord's house.

25 So Joshua spared Rahab the prostitute and her relatives who were with her in the house, because she had hidden the spies Joshua sent to Jericho. And she lives among the Israelites to this day."

To this day, no one has rebuilt Jericho. And this is why.

JOSHUA 6

26 "At that time Joshua invoked this curse:

"May the curse of the Lord fall on anyone

who tries to rebuild the town of Jericho.

At the cost of his firstborn son,

he will lay its foundation.

At the cost of his youngest son,

he will set up its gates."

Here is Jericho current day. Looks like everyone took the curse seriously.

Just like Revelation 18 says, judgment will fall and the criminal cabal will be consumed by fire, just like Jericho.

REVELATION 18

8 "Therefore, these plagues
will overtake her in a single day—
death and mourning and famine.
She will be completely consumed by fire,
for the Lord God who judges her is mighty."

9 And the kings of the world who committed adultery with her and enjoyed her great luxury will mourn for her as they see the smoke rising from her charred remains.

10 They will stand at a distance, terrified by her great torment."

And Revelation 19 joins in the celebration!

REVELATION 19

1 After this, I heard what sounded like a vast crowd in heaven shouting,
"Praise the Lord!
Salvation and glory and power belong to our God.
2 His judgments are true and just.
He has punished the great prostitute
who corrupted the earth with her immorality.
He has avenged the murder of his servants."
3 And again their voices rang out:
"Praise the Lord!
The smoke from that city ascends forever and ever!"

That, my fellow Patriots, is what we are about to see.

The Complete and Utter Decimation and Destruction of the New World Order AntiChrist Cabal.

Get Ready.

7 JAEL - ONE OF THE FIERCEST WARRIORS WAS A LADY!

I am going to take a wild guess that many of you have never heard this Biblical account tucked away in the Book of Judges. I don't recall ever hearing a sermon about it, but it's a doozy! This is a war time story Biblical account. It's not a bedtime story, so buckle up. But it really is insightful as to what we are experiencing as humanity.

So many Bible stories are being fulfilled before our eyes. This story is no different. The people did not rid Canaan of the Canaanite cannibals, as the LORD commanded. They lived nearby the Canaanites...they became friends...and some intermarried. Some even ended up joining in the evil Canaanite rituals! When God's people joined in the Baal worship, the LORD allowed them to fall under the rule of an evil king named Jabin. They had to learn a very difficult lesson. All of humanity is learning a very difficult lesson. Very few of us took seriously how evil and tricky the enemy is, and how satan's minions would take over these positions of authority to threaten our very existence. Very few of us have stood against this evil, and lived to tell about it. The Israelites found themselves under this tyrannical rule just as we have and found it to be just as unbearable as we do.

This is the story of Deborah and Jael (Ya-el). The people had been crying out to the LORD to save them from the Canaanite cannibals. Sounds familiar. The LORD sent a message to a military leader named Barak to attack King Jabin. But he didn't. He knew how ruthless the Canaanites were and he just couldn't bring himself to lead the people into battle.

Deborah, the judge of the Israelites, called Barak to speak to her. A judge in that day heard from the LORD and rendered decisions for the people. Deborah asked Barak why he had not gone into battle as the LORD told him to.

JUDGES 4

6 "One day she sent for Barak son of Abinoam, who lived in Kedesh in the land of Naphtali. She said to him, "This is what the Lord, the God of Israel, commands you: Call out 10,000 warriors from the tribes of Naphtali and Zebulun at Mount Tabor.

7 And I will call out Sisera, commander of Jabin's army, along with his chariots and warriors, to the Kishon River. There I will give you victory over him."

Barak said he wouldn't go fight the Canaanites unless Deborah went with him. He was just plain scared. In his defense, Barak knew how ruthless these Canaanites were. He knew how much they enjoyed torturing people. He knew they were filled with demons. But he also knew that Deborah heard from the LORD and would give His guidance in the battle. He knew if she lead the battle, they would defeat those demon worshipers. Many have underestimated the enemy we are fighting. They appear so normal. The dress so nicely. And speak so well. But as we have been told on the 17 board,

EPHESIANS 6

12 "We are not fighting against flesh-and-blood enemies, but against evil rulers and authorities of the unseen world, against mighty powers in this dark world, and against evil spirits in the heavenly places."

17 is not kidding.

Deborah agreed to go, and history recorded the battle was won by a woman.

JUDGES 4

9a "Very well," she replied, "I will go with you. But you will receive no honor in this venture, for the Lord's victory over Sisera will be at the hands of a woman."

Barak didn't care. He didn't care who got the recognition. He just wanted victory and for his warriors to not fall into the hands of these gruesome, ruthless demons.

The Battle against Jabin's Army was fought in the Jezreel Valley... also called the Valley of Megiddo. This rare flat area is near the center of Israel, and is symbolically the location for the Battle of Armageddon. (Of course, we know Armageddon is a digital/information war primarily on the airwaves.) Just as the LORD promised, the Israelites went to battle and quickly routed Jabin's forces and defeated them. Their commander, who I enjoy calling Sissy Sisera, ran away like a frightened rabbit! He ran as fast as he could across the Jezreel Valley and left his army in the dust! But he couldn't outrun God. His day of judgment had come and the LORD had him run directly into hell. That hell came by the name of a woman named Jael (Ya-el).

Jael was a rare warrior. She didn't go to the battlefield, but she sure did do battle that day. She was one cool operator. As the LORD would have it, Jael saw Sissy Sisera running across the Jezreel Valley and she directed him to her tent..."Oh come here! I will protect you!" she said.

Sissy Sisera fell right into her trap. Yael told him to hide under the blanket to make sure Barak didn't find him. He asked for water and Jael gave him milk and put him at ease. I have a feeling Yael spiked that milk with a sleeping potion because next thing you knew, Sissy Sisera was out like a light! And our amazing heroine Jael wasted no time. She grabbed one of her tent pegs and her trusty hammer and drove that tent peg right through Sissy Sisera's skull. Yes. That's what she did. The woman with nerves of steel killed the general of Jabin's army. What an amazing woman! What an amazing warrior!

Disinformation is necessary. She could've written the course on Sun Tzu war. She led Sissy Sisera right into her trap and he believed every word she said. Can you just imagine it? Sisera never imagined the trap she had laid for him. He just relaxed, hid under that blanket, and went night night. And he woke up in hell.

Deborah and Jael - two bold, female warriors – are the heroines of this battle. Well, how do you like that? In the Great and Final Battle of Armageddon, who would have figured that many of the strong, valiant warriors would be women? I really hadn't imagined what Armageddon would look like. But I love that we women can fight from our homes without going into a physical battlefield. We can destroy the enemy with one blow! With one social media post! Bam! The truth we are sharing is even mightier than a tent peg! With that truth we are nailing this entire evil, criminal mob through their skull!

I am sure that was not Jael's first time to use a tent peg and a hammer. She was a skilled warrior even though she had likely never trained for battle. I can imagine that Jael had prayed that she could somehow be part of helping set the people free from this brutal Canaanite regime. And the LORD answered her prayer. Just like each of us has prayed and is having a role in this great Battle of Armageddon!

After Jael killed Sisera, she didn't move a muscle. She stayed right by her tent. And when Barak came nearby, she let him know that the man they were looking for was in her tent with a tent peg through his skull. Deborah's prophecy came true.

JUDGES 4

9b *"the Lord's victory over Sisera will be at the hands of a woman..."*

Never doubt it. We are driving a stake through the skull of this evil, satanic New World Order criminal cabal. From the safety of our homes. It's quite a wonder, if you think about it. And a blessing.

The evil satanic cult is ghoulishly fascinated with the skull. How appropriate to crush the enemy's skull! They even wrote a song about Deborah and Jael! I'm sure it was quite a catchy tune. Here are some of the lyrics:

JUDGES 5

24"Most blessed among women is Jael,

the wife of Heber the Kenite.

May she be blessed above all women who live in tents.

25 Sisera asked for water,

and she gave him milk.

In a bowl fit for nobles,

she brought him yogurt.

26 Then with her left hand she reached for a tent peg,

and with her right hand for the workman's hammer.

She struck Sisera with the hammer, crushing his head.

With a shattering blow, she pierced his temples.

27 He sank, he fell,

he lay still at her feet.

And where he sank, there he died."

They sure don't make songs like they used to! One day songs will be written about how Patriots with nerves of steel fought valiantly day after day to defeat this Beast of Revelation and cast them into the pits of hell. The freedom and peace and joy that will settle over the entire earth will shock and amaze everyone, and put a song of victory in every heart. They will all want to know how this victory and peace was brought about...this Great

Kingdom of Christ on earth. Just watch and see.

One more interesting connection. Do you remember when David killed Goliath? He took Goliath's skull and buried it on the mountain of the LORD in Jerusalem. That was the very same mountain - at Golgotha - "The Place of the Skull" - where our LORD Jesus hung on the cross to die for our sins.

Jesus's cross on which He died was the tent peg that pierced through the skull of the enemy.

Because of what our LORD Jesus did, our victory over the enemy is sure.

> GENESIS 3
>
> 15 *"I will put hostility between you and the woman, and between your seed and her seed.* **He will strike your head,** *and* **you will strike his heel."**

Our LORD Jesus is the Victor!

He has dealt the enemy the fatal blow.

He is the Conqueror of the devil and his minions.

That is why nothing can stop what is coming.

8 GIDEON - NO FLEECE REQUIRED

Before the Great Awakening I thought our country just had a disagreement between our two main political parties. Yes...a serious disagreement. But I thought politicians were in those positions to represent their people and help them. Even though I greatly disagreed with what some of them stood for.

Silly me.

Silly silly silly me.

I have had to face the truth that for the vast majority of the politicians, that is simply not the case.

They serve many masters...the lobbyists, Big Pharma, Big Tech, their blackmailers, their bribers...their cabal bosses.

Most of our friends and family members have not swallowed down that nasty red pill. I still want to believe the people in these positions are independent-thinking, honorable public servants. I wish that were the case. But for one reason or another, they are controlled. Some are in on the scam to cheat Americans and get rich. Some are blackmailed. Some are useful idiots. One way or another most have been controlled and completely ineffective at representing the people.

That is not by accident. It is because a very powerful and sinister criminal machine placed them there intentionally to do their will, and this machine does not have our best interests in mind at all. Their plan is called Agenda 21, and they will not stop working toward that evil agenda until they are successful or they are brought to judgment. That is the only explanation for the incessant wars, the outrageous mounting debt, the election fraud, the failing and communistic education system, the culture degradation, the loss of our borders and our sovereignty, the intelligence community surveilling and controlling each citizen's every move through Big Tech, and the demoralizing injustice system.

None of this is by accident. Sinister forces have been moving humanity step by step by step to total tyranny. Elected officials have thus far been unwilling or unable to stop this progression. What would compel these people to inflict such abuse on humanity?

Baal.

Who's that, you ask?

Baal is literally the power of demons for political and financial gain.

That explains it.

And it is Biblical.

As old as the hills.

That's the only thing that explains the unbounded corruption everywhere.

We thought our troubles could be fixed through the election system or by legislation. But this criminal mafia has infiltrated every possible avenue for gaining justice. The swamp is far deeper and wider and more despicable than we ever imagined. We are fighting literal demons. The people we have trusted are led by demons. No wonder most of our family and friends won't swallow that red pill. It's a big one and it goes down hard. That's one of the main reasons Baal worship has been so successful for so long. Most people cannot or will not or don't want to believe it is true.

That brings us to the historical account of Gideon around 1154 BC.

The Bible records the sad history of the Israelites worshiping Baal with satanic sacrifices, just like the other nations did. Their leaders enticed them into the downward vortex of evil over and over again. We have learned how difficult it is to stand against the forces of darkness on every side. JFK's assassination by the CIA is case in point. It seems outrageous that anyone would participate in this vile evil practice. Clearly demon worship was very effective for gaining political and financial power, then and now.

But the LORD would not allow His people to be taken over by demons. He could have wiped the Israelites out, but He didn't. For the sake of His promises to Abraham, Isaac, and Jacob and His own good name, He didn't. He put the Israelites under the brutal rule of the Midianites who also worshiped Baal, to purge this evil from them. This time it was THEIR children that were sacrificed, and THAT jolted them awake.

The vast majority of humanity has had this evil purged from them and recoils in horror at the mere notion of Baal worship. That is very good news. God's plan to purge humanity of the demonic connection was successful. It only took about 3,000 years.

Gideon and his fellow Israelites were so tormented by the satan worshiping Midianites - for seven years - that they were forced to hide in caves to protect their family, and to hide their children from being abducted by these monsters for their horrifying rituals! Surviving was quite a challenge. Whenever the Israelites built up any assets, whether it was livestock or homes or crops, the Midianites would just come and take them away. Sound familiar?

Imagine the desperation.

Exactly what the LORD warned would happen if they worshipped Baal, happened.

The people cried to the LORD to save them.

After 20 long years, their prayers were answered. One day the Angel of the Lord appeared to Gideon.

Gideon was from the weakest tribe of Manasseh.

He was least in his entire family.

He didn't have a fancy position.

He didn't have a royal title.

Just like most of us.

How many times does the LORD use nobodies?

ALL the time.

Gideon is quite an interesting character. Picture this. Just trying to survive, Gideon hid his grain from the Midianites by threshing wheat at a winepress, of all places! All of a sudden, the Angel of the LORD appeared before Gideon and said "Mighty hero, the LORD is with you!" Gideon might not have felt like a mighty hero, hiding to thresh a little grain to survive. But Gideon was a hero to the LORD! Gideon didn't bow or tremble like others who saw the LORD. He was probably all trembled out! The Midianites had him and his friends half-starved. Gideon just wanted to understand why the LORD had abandoned them. The LORD didn't say, but I will. It was the Baal worship. Hello. The LORD didn't focus on their failures. He told Gideon to go and gather forces to fight the Midianites. What did Gideon do?

He told the Angel, "Please wait right here and I'm going to cook some dinner for you."

Of all the things I could think of to say, if ever I saw an angel, that would not be it. What's even funnier is that the Angel actually said He would wait. Gideon went home and literally slaughtered a goat, cooked it, and came back with the meal for the Angel of the LORD. How long could that have taken? Really, Gideon?! Gideon wanted a sign that the LORD would help them defeat these demons. When Gideon placed the food in front of the Angel, the Angel touched the food and it caught fire and was burned up. Then the Angel of the Lord disappeared. Now Gideon was flipping out! He realized he had not just seen an angel, but the literal LORD of heaven and earth. The "Angel of the LORD" is another term for the preincarnate Christ. Gideon was afraid he was going to die, but the LORD reassured him he was not.

With this newfound burst of courage to fight these horrible Baal worshipers, Gideon tore down his father's altar to Baal. In its place he built an altar to the LORD and sacrificed a bull to the LORD on it. When the Midianites found out, they were furious. Their altar was intended to conjure up demonic spirits...not heavenly spirits!

Gideon was still running on the fumes of his encounter with the Angel of the LORD, and he said that Baal should defend himself if he was so great! From that moment on Gideon was called Jerubbaal which means "Let Baal defend himself." Gideon was on fire!

Gideon immediately blew the ram's horn summoning warriors from all around. Thirty-two thousand warriors showed up! I think all those warriors looking at him put Gideon into shock, and his courage fizzled out! So he went before the LORD and asked for another sign. Gideon didn't need a sign. He needed to trust the plan. Wink. Wink.

Gideon laid out a fleece on the ground and asked the LORD to have the fleece remain wet and the ground dry. Just as Gideon asked, in the morning the fleece was soaking wet from the dew and the ground was completely dry. But poor Gideon began to think that was just a "coincidence." So he asked the LORD again. This time to leave the ground wet and the fleece dry. And that's exactly what happened. But poor Gideon scratched his head and wondered again if it was just another coincidence. Gideon was the most unlikely of leaders...and he was no scientist either.

Finally Gideon realized that he hadn't listened well enough in science class. But he knew that with God there are no coincidences, and that the LORD would be with them in battle, fleece or no fleece. And having faith was what the test was all about anyway.

Before it was over, the LORD would test Gideon's faith a lot more. Can I get an amen?

Many of us can relate to Gideon. One minute he was demolishing the altar of Baal and setting up God's altar and basically telling the prophets of Baal to shove it...and the next minute he was saying, "God are you going to be with me? Show me the fleece!" Faith is bigger than whether fleece is wet or dry. Faith is about sensing the LORD'S direction and following Him even when we don't know the next step. We know a bit about how Gideon felt.

Imagine you had 32,000 soldiers who were waiting for your command to lead them into battle. They were counting on you to lead them to victory and to keep them from getting killed! Gideon was determined to hear from the LORD and follow His instructions to the letter. The Lord told Gideon to do something so outrageous it could only be from God. You'd never find this military strategy in any war manual. The LORD had Gideon go to the soldiers and tell them if anyone was afraid they could head on home. What?! Have you ever heard of such? Think about it for a minute. Humanly speaking, we always want more resources, more money, more ammo, more warriors...

More!

More!!

MORE!!!!

But the LORD does not need that. He will win the battle and show everyone that He alone won the victory. Yes for His Glory...AND because He knows we need to know He is in control.

Our victory will be won with or without social media, or the mainstream media or any one ever believing a word we say.

God is in control.

After those who were scared went home, there were only 10,000 left in Gideon's army to go up against the 132,000 Midianites! The Bible doesn't say Gideon was worried. He didn't ask for another fleece sign. It would be interesting to know what Gideon was thinking. But the Bible doesn't tell us. Want to know what I think? I think Gideon was at the same point we are. He had had a bellyful of the Midianites' brutal tyranny. He couldn't take one more minute of hearing parents' desperate cries of anguish because their children had been abducted for the terrifying rituals to Baal. He had tried everything he could on his own. He was out of options. He had no plan, except for one. To trust God and His plan. That's where I am. How about you?

Then the LORD told Gideon he still had too many warriors! What?! The Midianites outnumbered the Israelites 13 to one! But Gideon knew about Moses and the 10 plagues on Egypt. He knew about the parting of the Red Sea. He knew how the walls of Jericho came tumbling down. So as impossible as it sounded, Gideon trusted the plan. The LORD told Gideon to send the men to the spring for water. All those who put their mouths in the water to drink like a dog were sent to one side, and all those who cupped the water in their hands were sent to the other side. Only 300 cupped the water in their hands...and those were God's chosen warriors against the Midianites. Only 300 Israelites would go fight against 132,000 Midianites!

The 300 Israelites were ready to fight, but they knew they would need the LORD to do a miracle to rescue them, because fighting the Midianites was like fighting demons straight from hell. They needed a miracle from the LORD and they knew it. Just like us. Put yourself in Gideon's shoes. Gideon knew the LORD had been directing him. So He trusted the LORD. Even though Gideon didn't ask, the LORD knew he need a boost of encouragement. So the LORD said,

JUDGES 7

9 "That night the Lord said, "Get up! Go down into the Midianite camp, for I have given you victory over them! 10 If you are afraid to attack, go down to the camp with your servant Purah.

11 Listen to what the Midianites are saying, and you will be greatly encouraged. Then you will be eager to attack."

When Gideon and Purah came near to the Midianite camp, they overheard two soldiers talking. Those soldiers talked about having a bad dream about Gideon's army.

JUDGES 7

13b "The man said, "I had this dream, and in my dream a loaf of barley bread came tumbling down into the Midianite camp. It hit a tent, turned it over, and knocked it flat!"

14 His companion answered, "Your dream can mean only one thing—God has given Gideon son of Joash, the Israelite, victory over Midian and all its allies!"

Yes the LORD gave the Midianites that dream. And He also caused them to see it as a sign of their defeat. The LORD struck fear in their hearts that Gideon was going to destroy them, and they couldn't shake that fear. So Gideon returned to camp filled with hope and encouragement that the LORD would give them victory over their enemies!

We see that happening with the New World Order. Their fear and panic has caused them to make very foolish moves that have exposed them before all the world. We've had a few glimpses into how the cabal really feels and they are petrified. They are in full panic that their destruction is near. On top of that, President Trump recently posted a video about the Nuremberg trials where the criminals were read the verdict over and over..."death by hanging, death by hanging, death by hanging." On that very same day Elon Musk posted on Twitter the law code about treason. Their nightmares are becoming reality. What a sight to behold!

Here's where I love the story of Gideon most. You are going to see how this historical account is being played out in our day! Gideon prepared his 300 warriors to go fight the Midianites. Gideon didn't give them typical battle gear like swords and spears and shields. Oh no. This battle was the LORD'S and He instructed Gideon to give each of the 300 warriors only three items.

A clay pot.

A torch.

And a trumpet.

That certainly was not from any military manual that has ever been written! This was an amazing plan that only the LORD of heaven and earth could create. At night, the 300 warriors were instructed to tiptoe very quietly around the Midianite encampment until they surrounded it. Once they were in place, the warriors were to wait for Gideon's signal and then they would crash their clay pot, revealing the torch inside, and blast their trumpet loudly right into the middle of the Midianite camp! Can you imagine? The Midianite soldiers woke up with a jolt from the loud crash of all those clay pots. They were completely disoriented by the 300 trumpets blasting in their ears, and from every direction they looked they saw the blazing fire of the torches all around them. Between the fear that the LORD put in their hearts, and the confusion from all of the noise and the torches, the Midianite soldiers <u>began to kill each other</u>!

Wow! What a plan straight from the LORD! The Midianites who weren't killed by their fellow soldiers, ran for their lives. They were chased by the other warriors who had not been part of the chosen 300.

JUDGES 7

22b *"Those who were not killed fled to places as far away as Beth-shittah near Zererah and to the border of Abel-meholah near Tabbath.*

23 *Then Gideon sent for the warriors of Naphtali, Asher, and Manasseh, who joined in chasing the army of Midian.*

24a *Gideon also sent messengers throughout the hill country of Ephraim, saying, "Come down to attack the Midianites. Cut them off at the shallow crossings of the Jordan River at Beth-barah..."*

This map shows where the Judges of Israel fought the Canaanites.

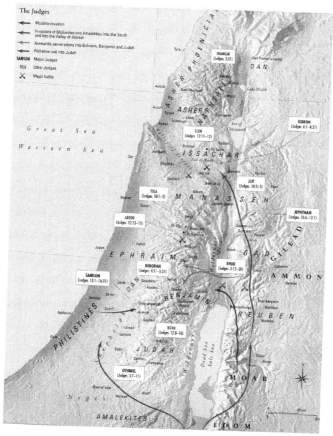

Not one hair was hurt on the head of any of Gideon's soldiers! They defeated the Midianites by

-shining the light,

-making lots of noise, and

-blasting the trumpet!

How Biblical is that?!

That's exactly what we're doing, Patriots!

We are making lots of noise!

We are shining the light of truth in every dark place, exposing every lie!

And we are blasting the trumpet of God's Word!

And of course we will win the victory with our wonderful President *Trump*! Does anyone else see the Biblical significance of the most hated man in the world, and most loved man in the world, being called TRUMP?

I have known the Bible story of Gideon for a very long time, but I never imagined that's how we would win the literal Battle of Armageddon. As we listen to the LORD and trust His plan, not one hair on our heads will be hurt. We will shine the light of truth, make lots of noise, and blast the trumpet of God's Word...and <u>the New World Order will destroy each other</u>!

They have always worked together in lock step. There has always seemed to be an ironclad brotherhood arrangement. Of course, the threat of having your tongue cut out if you ever tell their secrets might have something to do with it. But I can imagine, that as the band of evil brothers breaks apart as one by one they turn state's evidence, it will be "every many for himself!" And when they don't know who to trust, their entire house of cards collapses!

On the other hand, we are banded together in this fight to save humanity. None of us will stop until we achieve victory. They continually try to incite us to violence, but Patriots all over the world refuse to play into their hands. Patriots all over the world are following the LORD'S plan on how to defeat this enemy and it is working! We are all listening to Him, and following His leading, and trusting His plan. Watch, and we will see our enemies destroy each other just like Gideon did!

9 SAMSON - PULLING DOWN THE TWO COLUMNS

I really think we've been all wrong about Samson. Hear me out. Samson was a fighter. He was born to destroy the Philistines. The LORD gave Samson superhuman strength for that one purpose. And having the unique calling on his life, Samson would stop at nothing to fulfill his destiny. Most people can't imagine that kind of inescapable, all-consuming calling. The warriors who fight every day in this Great Battle of Armageddon have an inkling how Samson felt. And Samson was victorious! He brought the whole diseased corrupt temple of Dagon down on the heads of the Philistine "elite" of his day! No doubt, the story of Samson is being fulfilled in our day. Samson has gotten a bad rap as a womanizer and a misogynist and a xenophobe and every other bad trait Hillary could criticize. You're going to love learning the truth about Samson!

Samson's mother could not conceive until one day an Angel of the LORD came to her and announced she was going to have a miracle son. The angel gave her very special instructions never to cut his hair and he should never drink alcohol. He was going to be a fighter, and would set God's people free from their Philistine enemies! When you think of Philistines, think Baal worshipers. The evil Philistines would come to a village and take whatever child they wanted for their evil sacrifices. Think of the cartels in Mexico and you'll be pretty close to who the Philistines were.

So in order to destroy the Philistines, Samson was going to have to be smart. Samson would be a bit rough around the edges...and very tricky. He would have to play 4-D Chess! (And I don't think

Chess had even been invented yet!) This was literally Samson's destiny...to destroy the evil Philistines.

When Samson was old enough to marry, he chose a Philistine girl. His parents were shocked. But who else would Samson choose to marry? How else could he infiltrate the Philistines to destroy them? Samson's parents were terrific...but they did not have the calling on their lives that Samson had. They could not understand the strategy and the planning and the attention and focus to complete this mission that was on Samson's life from the get-go. The honest truth is, I don't really think Samson was that much of a womanizer. But he used that persona to trick the Philistines. They thought Samson was one of them. They thought he was a fool, so they let their guard down. Do you know what? This Samson guy reminds me of somebody else I know who is very, very tricky. Someone who has fooled all the Deep State cabal Philistines of our day. Someone who made himself out to be womanizer. Any guesses?

Here are a few hints.

Just as the Angel foretold, Samson didn't drink alcohol. That's not typical. Check.

And Samson had long hair. Who do we know with unusually long hair? Check.

And Samson was outrageously strong. One of the historical accounts in Judges Chapter 16 records that Samson killed 1,000 Philistines in one fight! With a jawbone of a **donkey**!

JUDGES 15

14 "As Samson arrived at Lehi, the Philistines came shouting in triumph. But the Spirit of the Lord came powerfully upon Samson, and he snapped the ropes on his arms as if they were burnt strands of flax, and they fell from his wrists.

15 Then he found the jawbone of a recently killed donkey. He picked it up and killed 1,000 Philistines with it.

16 Then Samson said,

"With the jawbone of a donkey,
I've piled them in heaps!
With the jawbone of a donkey,
I've killed a thousand men!"

Samson didn't use an AR-15!

He didn't use a sword!

His weapon was a jawbone of all things!

A **donkey's** jawbone!

Anyone seeing some symbolism here?!

Anybody think of someone who is destroying evildoers of our day with the flapping jawbone of these Democrat donkeys?

President Trump IS Samson!

There is just so much symbolism you can't miss it! There are just too many coincidences.

Whenever I've thought of Samson, I've thought Samson was a strong character and a valiant fighter, but it was a shame that he couldn't overcome his temptation with women. Women were his downfall. But do you know what? I think I was wrong. I really do think Samson strategically played this role, and put himself in this dangerous position, using Delilah, for one purpose and one purpose only. To destroy the Philistines. That was his mission and nothing stood in the way of Samson accomplishing that mission.

Remember that Samson was a Nazirite and was under God's mandate never to cut his hair? And he never did, by all accounts. As he fulfilled his mission, his strength grew and grew and grew, along with his hair. So what if Samson hooked up with Delilah because he knew she was a no account dirty dog opportunist?! She was the original gold digger! And Samson knew that whatever he told her, she would go straight back and tell his enemies. This sounds so crazy to you and me. Just as crazy as some of the things we've seen President Trump do to draw out the criminals! When something President Trump does or says doesn't add up, you know he is pulling a Samson! It happens time and again, and some people turn on him, because they don't understand what he's doing. They don't understand Sun Tzu war. He's always taking the slings and arrows because he actually draws out their slings and arrows on purpose! How else would he expose them so we can see through their masquerade!

President Trump, our Samson, is bound and determined to destroy the New World Order cabal and nothing will get in the way of that mission. He doesn't care what he must do, or what price he must pay, or what abuse he must take...He WILL fulfill that mission.

As the story of Samson goes, he played Delilah like a fiddle. It's always struck me as outrageously stupid that Samson would play along with Delilah, and then give up his secret about never cutting his hair, when he knew that woman could not be trusted! Either Delilah was extremely enticing, or...Samson was using her to get to his enemies. Samson was playing a very dangerous game of chess. But he knew that was the only way to destroy God's enemies. Remind you of another courageous Chess player? God's chosen warriors are smart and strong and courageous. Here is how crybaby Delilah whined her way to discover Samson's secret.

JUDGES 16

4 *"Some time later Samson fell in love with a woman named Delilah, who lived in the valley of Sorek.*

5 *The rulers of the Philistines went to her and said, "Entice Samson to tell you what makes him so strong and how he can be overpowered and tied up securely. Then each of us will give you 1,100 pieces of silver."*

6 So Delilah said to Samson, "Please tell me what makes you so strong and what it would take to tie you up securely."

7 Samson replied, "If I were tied up with seven new bowstrings that have not yet been dried, I would become as weak as anyone else."

8 So the Philistine rulers brought Delilah seven new bowstrings, and she tied Samson up with them. 9 She had hidden some men in one of the inner rooms of her house, and she cried out, "Samson! The Philistines have come to capture you!" But Samson snapped the bowstrings as a piece of string snaps when it is burned by a fire. So the secret of his strength was not discovered.

10 Afterward Delilah said to him, "You've been making fun of me and telling me lies! Now please tell me how you can be tied up securely."

11 Samson replied, "If I were tied up with brand-new ropes that had never been used, I would become as weak as anyone else."

12 So Delilah took new ropes and tied him up with them. The men were hiding in the inner room as before, and again Delilah cried out, "Samson! The Philistines have come to capture you!" But again Samson snapped the ropes from his arms as if they were thread.

13 Then Delilah said, "You've been making fun of me and telling me lies! Now tell me how you can be tied up securely." Samson replied, "If you were to weave the seven braids of my hair into the fabric on your loom and tighten it with the loom shuttle, I would become as weak as anyone else."

So while he slept, Delilah wove the seven braids of his hair into the fabric.

14 Then she tightened it with the loom shuttle. Again she cried out, "Samson! The Philistines have come to capture you!" But Samson woke up, pulled back the loom shuttle, and yanked his hair away from the loom and the fabric.

15 Then Delilah pouted, "How can you tell me, 'I love you,' when

113

you don't share your secrets with me? You've made fun of me three times now, and you still haven't told me what makes you so strong!" 16 She tormented him with her nagging day after day until he was sick to death of it.

17 Finally, Samson shared his secret with her. "My hair has never been cut," he confessed, "for I was dedicated to God as a Nazirite from birth. If my head were shaved, my strength would leave me, and I would become as weak as anyone else."

18 Delilah realized he had finally told her the truth, so she sent for the Philistine rulers. "Come back one more time," she said, "for he has finally told me his secret." So the Philistine rulers returned with the money in their hands.

19 Delilah lulled Samson to sleep with his head in her lap, and then she called in a man to shave off the seven locks of his hair. In this way she began to bring him down, and his strength left him.

20 Then she cried out, "Samson! The Philistines have come to capture you!" When he woke up, he thought, "I will do as before and shake myself free." But he didn't realize the Lord had left him.

21 So the Philistines captured him and gouged out his eyes. They took him to Gaza, where he was bound with bronze chains and forced to grind grain in the prison."

Let's be honest. Nobody is **that** enticing. And nobody is **that** stupid. Certainly not Samson.

The story of Samson is not a moral tale about how you should not sleep around, and it's not a lesson about dating advice. It's about a man on a mission.

Of course, we all know the story. And every time we read it we shout, "No Samson! Don't tell her your secret!" And every time, he tells her that he will lose his strength if his hair is cut. And the woman does it! She literally cuts his hair! And then she calls his enemies to come and arrest him and throw him in prison! Want to know what I wonder? I wonder if he willingly lost his power and strength. I wonder if Samson was just biding (Biden) his time...lying in wait...for just the right moment...until his hair grew back and he had the opportunity to annihilate his enemies?

Just look at all the parallels! Look at what happened to President Trump. He was seemingly so strong! He was the President of the United States of America! He made America great again! Twice! The people adored him! He was solving world crises right and left! The man had superhuman Samson-like strength! And he did it with a jawbone of a donkey!

But then he willingly stepped down, by all appearances. (Even though we all know what is happening behind the scenes.) Did President Trump fool everyone...by willingly being removed from power...while not losing his power at all? We are all awaiting his great comeback, when he says we will be very happy! Remember how Samson's victory went?

JUDGES 16

23 "The Philistine rulers held a great festival, offering sacrifices and praising their god, Dagon. They said, "Our god has given us victory over our enemy Samson!"

24 When the people saw him, they praised their god, saying, "Our god has delivered our enemy to us! The one who killed so many of us is now in our power!"

25 Half drunk by now, the people demanded, "Bring out Samson so he can amuse us!" So he was brought from the prison to amuse them, and they had him stand between the pillars supporting the roof.

26 Samson said to the young servant who was leading him by the hand, "Place my hands against the pillars that hold up the temple. I want to rest against them."

27 Now the temple was completely filled with people. All the

Philistine rulers were there, and there were about 3,000 men and women on the roof who were watching as Samson amused them."

The Philistine elite gathered for one of their "festivals" at the Dagon temple to celebrate their omnibus bill or some other theft of the people. No doubt they were doing their evil demonic sacrifices, and to add to their fun, they had Samson brought out of prison so they could make sport of him. He appeared weak and pitiful...and they laughed and drank and drank and laughed. But the Word of God says Samson's strength was back. He was just fooling them! Samson asked the guards to put him between two columns so he could rest against them, because he was so, so weak. Samson was milking it for all it was worth! Then Samson waited until they were all good and sauced! He knew his time of revenge had arrived.

The stage was set.

All of the evil Philistine "elite" were under one roof.

They were too drunk to stop him.

This was the moment Samson could bring down their entire house of cards!

JUDGES 16

28 "Then Samson prayed to the Lord, "Sovereign Lord, remember me again. O God, please strengthen me just one more time. With one blow let me pay back the Philistines for the loss of my two eyes."

29 Then Samson put his hands on the two center pillars that held up the temple. Pushing against them with both hands,

30 he prayed, "Let me die with the Philistines." And the temple crashed down on the Philistine rulers and all the people. So he killed more people when he died than he had during his entire lifetime."

Samson began to push those two center columns...those two columns which represent the infiltrated Church and the infiltrated State...like the Masonic columns the cabal has used to build their evil society with secret handshakes and secret deals. We will bring those two columns down and set the Church and the State free to do the work to bring peace and healing on the earth.

Suddenly, as Samson pushed, the columns loosened from their footings. The supports and the roof above started to crumble. Samson kept pushing and pushing, and it seems no one was sober enough to stop him. All at once the entire structure came down on their heads! All the "elite" Philistines were crushed and destroyed. The Bible says that Samson destroyed more enemies on that day than he had destroyed in his entire life. All these demon worshipers were destroyed in one fell swoop! Mission accomplished!

That is what President Trump and the Patriots are going to do. We are going to bring this whole bleeping diseased corrupt temple down on their heads. Just like 17 said. Make no mistake about it.

The NWO Philistines will be destroyed just like the Philistines of Samson's day. The two columns - the Church and the State - that they infiltrated and hijacked for their own gain and corruption, will be completely destroyed. All these corrupt usurping infil-TRAITORS will be crushed. That is what the story of Samson is all about.

And then the true Church and the true State will be restored to their rightful place, lead by righteous leaders. It is happening already, and will be completed. Then President Trump and all of humanity will laugh and laugh and laugh!

10 DAVID - SLAYING THE GOLIATH WORLD ORDER

After it became obvious that the judges and prophets were not able to establish a free and just society, the people had a hankering for a king. The LORD told them they didn't need a king. He told them all would go well, if they would just follow Him. But no. They wanted a king. The LORD told them a king would just tax them and send their sons to war. But no. They wanted a king. And a king is what they got. The first king out of the gate was pathetic. More about him later. This story is about someone who had the makings of a wonderful king! Because he had the courage to fight the giant enemies of God's people.

At first blush this story seems simple.

Humanity is David...seemingly powerless to stop this gigantic behemoth Goliath New World Order that controls all these positions of power over us.

But David miraculously defeats the Goliath NWO!
Hurray!
End of story.
But there's more.

How did humanity get into this mess where Goliath rules the world? (By the way, Goliath means "a large and powerful organization.")
Also known as the New World Order.
Also known as the Globalist Central Banking Mafia Cartel.
Also known as the Illuminati.
Also known as the Beast of Revelation.
Also known as the AntiChrist.

First of all, when God's people do nothing, or cower in fear, the evildoers take over. That has happened in every country, every state, every town, every school district, and every city council...all over the world. As the famous saying goes, all that needs to happen for evil to triumph is for good people to do nothing. And the less we do, the more likely it is we won't do anything. We will cower in fear, and fear becomes our worst enemy. Even worse than Goliath. Goliath will taunt and curse and threaten. And steal and cheat and kill to get power and keep it. And ultimately enslave humanity.

There's another tyrant in the story. His name was Saul. Saul was chosen to be the king, but he was weak and pathetic and greedy. Like most of our politicians. Long before this toe-to-toe with Goliath, it was painfully obvious that Saul was not up to the challenge of being king of God's people. Remember, the LORD never wanted the people to have a king anyway. The LORD is our king. He wanted to lead His people through the prophets and judges, who would tell them what God wanted them to do and He would protect them. But no. Our ancestors wanted to be like everyone else. So the LORD finally let them. Saul was anointed king. And just as the LORD warned, they ended up enslaved. Taxed. Always sending their young men to fight in battle. History has been a never-ending series of one battle and then another and another and another. The tyrants gained more power and wealth, and the people ended up under their boots.

Saul, if he were a good king, would be leading the charge into battle against Goliath, but where do we find him? Safe in his tent behind the lines of his soldiers, wringing his hands, cowering in fear. What Saul didn't know was that months prior, the prophet Samuel had gone to the home of Jesse in Bethlehem, and anointed a young shepherd boy named David to be the next king. David was anointed with oil. He was "The Chosen One."

Why did the LORD choose David? Besides the fact that Saul was worthless as a king, the LORD chose David because the LORD does not see as man sees. The Bible says,

1st SAMUEL 16

7 *"The Lord doesn't see things the way you see them. People judge by outward appearance, but the Lord looks at the heart."*

David was from a little nowhere town, in a nobody family. And besides that, he was the youngest of the family, and he had the lowly job of tending the sheep. Well, here's a shocker...those were the exact qualities the LORD was looking for in the next king! All those nights out in the silent, in the cold, in the dark, in the loneliness, in the dangerous, David was becoming the man Israel needed to lead them. So if you feel that you're in a nowhere town from a nobody family, and that no one shows you any never mind, be encouraged by the story of David. The LORD has great plans for those who faithfully do His will, when it seems that no one notices.

The story begins with David's brothers criticizing him...

(I seem to see a pattern here. Just like Joseph was despised by his brothers, anyone who stands for righteousness and does the right thing, is going to catch a lot of grief. Usually the criticism comes from those who are lazy and evil. Didn't they remember Samuel anointed David? Looks like they were jealous of David, just like Joseph's brothers were jealous of him.)

During the war between Israel and the Philistines, David stayed with his father, Jesse, to tend the sheep just as he had been told, while his brothers went to battle. David's father told him to go check on his brothers in the battle and to report back.

When David appeared at the battle site, it didn't take his brothers long to start criticizing David for simply obeying their father. And it didn't take long for David to hear the taunts of wicked, arrogant Goliath. I can just see it. David came upon this amazing scene of two armies arrayed for battle, catches grief from his rude insolent brothers, and then hears the rude insults against the LORD, from Goliath. It's hard to distinguish between his brothers and Goliath!

1st SAMUEL 17

8b "I am the Philistine champion, but you are only the servants of Saul. Choose one man to come down here and fight me! 9 If he kills me, then we will be your slaves. But if I kill him, you will be our slaves! 10 I defy the armies of Israel today! Send me a man who will fight me!" 11 When Saul and the Israelites heard this, they were terrified and deeply shaken."

David was so angry to hear this wicked Goliath spew these insults against the LORD and His people. And then David looked over at the miserable excuse of an army...a frightened bunch of cowards. David couldn't take it for five minutes. Day after day after day the "soldiers" had come to the battlefield, supposedly to fight, and they did nothing. They would go back to camp and do it over and over again, day after day after day after day. David was beside himself!

David told them:

1st SAMUEL 17

26b "Who is this pagan Philistine anyway, that he is allowed to defy the armies of the living God?"

In other words, "What is wrong with you people? Get off your behinds and fight for crying out loud! How could you let this pagan jackal speak of the LORD and His army that way?"

But it was useless. The people were paralyzed with fear. All they could see was how big Goliath was and that prevented them from seeing how great and awesome the LORD is. And that's what I love about David. David would spend night after night in the quiet, always sleeping with one eye open to protect the sheep. He would risk his life daily. Literally every day, David would fight a bear or a lion or any enemy that came his way and he would protect those sheep. That is why the LORD chose

David. This is the exact character we need for good leaders in our country. We don't need those who cower in fear. We need fighters. We need those who are willing to risk their lives and money and their names for the good of others. We need those who have clear eyes to see what to do and have the courage to do it!

There was no use talking to those lily-livered cowards, so off David went to see the king. He wasted no time volunteering to fight the enemy of the LORD. David did not concern himself with his size or his age or his experience. He had his eye on the LORD and he was going to fight the battle and defeat Goliath in the name of the LORD, and that was all there was to it.

1ˢᵗ SAMUEL 17

32 "Don't worry about this Philistine," David told Saul. "I'll go fight him!"

33 "Don't be ridiculous!" Saul replied. "There's no way you can fight this Philistine and possibly win! You're only a boy, and he's been a man of war since his youth."

34 But David persisted. "I have been taking care of my father's sheep and goats," he said. "When a lion or a bear comes to steal a lamb from the flock, 35 I go after it with a club and rescue the lamb from its mouth. If the animal turns on me, I catch it by the jaw and club it to death. 36 I have done this to both lions and bears, and I'll do it to this pagan Philistine, too, for he has defied the armies of the living God!

37a The Lord who rescued me from the claws of the lion and the bear will rescue me from this Philistine!"

When Saul tried to discourage David, he remembered how the LORD had helped him before, and trusted the LORD would help him this time too! Each of us has fought for righteousness in one way or another, countless times, and we aren't afraid! The LORD will see us through to victory!

Did you hear how the LORD prepared David? David would chase after a lion or bear and rescue one of his lambs from its mouth! David carried a club and would grab a lion or a bear by the jaw and club it to death! So David was confident he could do the same to that pagan Philistine Goliath! Wow! All that David had experienced, prepared him for the day of battle...much like us, Patriots! The Lord has prepared you for this day, so Let's Go!

1ˢᵗ SAMUEL 17

37b "Saul finally consented. "All right, go ahead," he said. "And may the Lord be with you!"

The shame of it all is that Saul let him do it!! How embarrassing! Isn't that exactly how it is, Patriots? We have paid these politicians good money to be in these positions to rule rightly, whether they are judges or congressman or state senators, or election officials, or you name it! Most have done nothing to protect us from the tyrants. They have become part of the problem! Our enemies are within! President Trump told us our enemies are not only foreign, but primarily domestic! These good-for-nothings have willingly put us in harm's way!

But just look at David! He has nothing! He wasn't getting paid for this! He wasn't trained for that! He wasn't supposed to have to do that job! But the sad truth is that nobody who was getting paid to do it, would! Sound familiar, Patriots? We are having to do the job that these sorry mainstream media, government officials, and supposed leaders have failed to do. I think we know a bit about how David felt.

The enemies of the LORD are taunting us and we will not put up with it for five more minutes.

We don't want your armor.
We don't want your mail.
We don't want your sword.
We don't want your shield.

We hear the taunts of the enemy every single day!

We do not care what they say.

We will go and fight in the name of the LORD.

I don't think David had been at the battlefield for very long from the time he arrived until the time he went out to meet Goliath. David had that fire burning in his belly...and he was going to put a stop to Goliath's big, foul, pagan mouth!

Check out what happened when David went out to face down Goliath.

1st SAMUEL 17

41 "Goliath walked out toward David with his shield-bearer ahead of him,

42 sneering in contempt at this ruddy-faced boy.

43 "Am I a dog," he roared at David, "that you come at me with a stick?" And he cursed David by the names of his gods.

44 "Come over here, and I'll give your flesh to the birds and wild animals!" Goliath yelled."

David didn't pay any attention to Goliath's sneers.
He didn't pay any attention to Goliath's curses.
He didn't pay any attention to Goliath's threats.

1st SAMUEL 17

45 "David replied to the Philistine, "You come to me with sword, spear, and javelin, but I come to you in the name of the Lord of Heaven's Armies—the God of the armies of Israel, whom you have defied.

46 Today the Lord will conquer you, and I will kill you and cut off your head. And then I will give the dead bodies of your men to the birds and wild animals, and the whole world will know that there is a God in Israel."

47 And everyone assembled here will know that the Lord rescues his people, but not with sword and spear. This is the Lord's battle, and he will give you to us!"

Quite the response from a young shepherd boy.

"I will kill you,

cut off your head,

and feed your dead body to the birds and wild animals."

Any questions?

David didn't waver.

He didn't flinch.

And He gave the glory to the LORD.

1st SAMUEL 17

48 "As Goliath moved closer to attack, David quickly ran out to meet him.

49 Reaching into his shepherd's bag and taking out a stone, he hurled it with his sling and hit the Philistine in the forehead. The stone sank in, and Goliath stumbled and fell face down on the ground.

50 So David triumphed over the Philistine with only a sling and a stone, for he had no sword.

51 Then David ran over and pulled Goliath's sword from its sheath. David used it to kill him and cut off his head."

David rushed out to meet Goliath.

No glory hogging.

No indecision.

David charged into battle like a wild bull!

He couldn't wait to shut up this worthless demon!

David was quicker on his feet than Goliath and had perfected his slingshot skills.

The LORD had prepared David for this very moment.

Goliath didn't stand a chance!

Just like David, we say, "New World Order, this day we will feed your body to the birds! We come to fight you in the name of the LORD of Heaven's armies!" We rush out into the battle just like David did! Every day we cast stones right into their watermelon heads, and knock them down to their knees to bow before the LORD! Whenever news breaks, we digital soldiers rush into battle to research and spread the truth on social media. With one post, we destroy their lies and they end up doing a face-plant! They thought their Goliath mainstream media and social media would do all the fighting for them. They weren't prepared for an army of digital soldiers slinging knockout posts right in their face!

The Israelites couldn't believe it either!

David did it!

He **really** did it!

He brought that braggadocious, arrogant, demon worshiping Goliath to his knees! With one stone! How could little David bring down this giant with a small stone? The same way we are destroying the New World Order with a tweet, with a post, with an email, with a text, and with a video! But how? Because TRUTH in the hands of the LORD of Heavens armies is powerful. He is directing those tweets, and truths, and texts, and emails straight to the head of this Beast! Oh yeah David did it. And we will do it too!

One of my favorite parts is when Saul found out that David really did kill Goliath and asked, "Who is this?"

Same for us.

The Deep State cabal bloodline Rotties still don't understand how we have this power!

"Who are these people?"

They just can't understand it.

Humanity has never been able to fight them like this.

ZECHARIAH 12

4 "On that day," says the Lord, "I will cause every horse to panic and every rider to lose his nerve. I will watch over the people of Judah, but I will blind all the horses of their enemies.

5 And the clans of Judah will say to themselves,

'The people of Jerusalem have found strength in the Lord of Heaven's Armies, their God.'"

Yes we certainly have. We have found strength in the LORD of Heaven's Armies, our God!

When David was summoned to Saul, the Bible says he still had Goliath's head in his clenched fist! Can you just imagine? He was still carrying Goliath's bloody head! The head of Goliath was David's trophy!

The head of the New World Order cabal is **our** trophy!

We will take their very own sword that they intended to use to destroy us, i.e. social media, and we will cut off their power and authority! We will swing right around just as David did, displaying their shame and destruction in our clenched fists!

This historical account from God's Word, is playing out worldwide for everyone to see. President Trump and we Patriots are David, and we are destroying the New World Order criminal mafia cabal Goliath. Do you see why I HAD to write this book? Every Bible story is being re-enacted before the world, and these stories give us a road map to where we are headed.

VINCERO!

VICTORY!

One day the LORD will pull out a huge scroll and open it, and testify that we were His chosen warriors for this Great Battle of Armageddon.

MALACHI 3

*16 "Then those who feared the Lord spoke with each other, and the Lord listened to what they said. **In his presence, a scroll of remembrance was written to record the names of those who feared him and always thought about the honor of his name.**"*

Our names will be in that scroll, as warriors who fought alongside Him to destroy the enemy of all time! Woah.

MALACHI 3

*17 "They will be my people," says the Lord of Heaven's Armies. "On the day when I act in judgment, they will be **my own special treasure**. I will spare them as a father spares an obedient child."*

Yep...that's us! We are His special TREASURE!

For all time, we will sing a song that no one will know except for those of us who fought in this worldwide Battle of Armageddon. As Revelation 14 describes, the 144,000 are those chosen knights who have the distinct honor and pleasure of fighting in the Army of the Living God, to destroy the New World Order Beast Goliath, in the strength of the LORD!

REVELATION 14

1 "Then I saw the Lamb standing on Mount Zion, and with him were 144,000 who had his name and his Father's name written on their foreheads.

2 And I heard a sound from heaven like the roar of mighty ocean waves or the rolling of loud thunder. It was like the sound of many harpists playing together.

3 This great choir sang a wonderful new song in front of the throne of God and before the four living beings and the twenty-four elders. No one could learn this song except the 144,000 who had been redeemed from the earth.

4 They have kept themselves as pure as virgins, following the Lamb wherever he goes. They have been purchased from among the people on the earth as a special offering to God and to the Lamb.

5 They have told no lies; they are without blame."

As 17 said, feel proud.

11 BALAAM - A PROPHET FOR PROFIT

The Bible doesn't really have that many funny stories. Most of the historical accounts are about tyrants taking over, and the people crying to the LORD for help, and the LORD rescuing them from their enemies. Not a lot to laugh about on any of that. But if you ask most anyone who has studied God's Word, "What is the funniest story in the Bible?" likely they will respond with the story of Balaam and his donkey. And it is funny! Except for the fact that Balaam is such a sorry excuse for a prophet. Nothing funny about that.

The story about Balaam is the story about a false prophet. And we've got a heaping helping of false prophets in our day. But I'll get to that in a minute. First of all, what self-respecting mother would ever name her child Balaam? Sounds like Baal-I am! I just can't imagine an Israelite mother giving her child that name. Do you know what I think? I bet that was his Cabal name because that's how they knew Balaam would do their bidding. But not this time. The story goes that the Moabites were afraid of the Israelites and they knew if a curse was placed on the Israelites, they would be safe. Some people might not believe in blessings and cursings, but they are real. And the Moabites certainly believed in it.

So who are you gonna call when you need a curse proclaimed on the Israelites?

Balaam.

The Bible doesn't say, but likely Balaam had helped the Moabites out before. He probably ran a side business "Curses R Us." The

Moabite emissaries came to the door and asked Balaam to help them out with a curse or two on the Israelites and he said he would have to ask the LORD. Of course, he had to at least "pretend" to be devout. The LORD told Balaam not to go, and to Balaam's credit he sent the Moabite emissaries away. The Moabite leader, Balak, was not deterred. He sent a bigger consort of emissaries to knock on Balaam's door saying they had an extra large sack of money and for him to come right away to curse the Israelites. The next conversation between Balaam and the LORD was very odd. Balaam asked the LORD if he should go. Balaam had already asked the LORD before, and the LORD had said no. Balaam didn't need to ask again. It's like when your child keeps asking to do something over and over and over. You've told them no. But they are bound and determined to do it. So to teach the child a lesson, you might relent and let him go.

That brings me to the point of why this story of Balaam is in this book about Bible stories being fulfilled before our eyes. Well...the sad truth is that there are many false prophets in our day. There are many who claim the name of the LORD as one of His messengers. But these people have two masters. They claim to want to do what God says, but they also want to do what makes a load of money. Many have been willing to say whatever they were told to say, just to keep their good paying jobs. I'm sorry. But that is the fact. Many preachers shut down their churches during Covid because the government said so. Many preachers encouraged their people to be obedient to the government and get the jab. Many preachers are frightening people with the cabal narrative that has been pummeled through the Soros-paid seminaries about the 666 and the Mark of the Beast and the world falling to the Beast. Many have not stood against the degradation of our society regarding abortion, or homosexuality, or transgender etc. And look where we are. (I understand that our hormones have been horribly manipulated, along with social media propaganda, and that has caused tremendous gender confusion, but that could be discussed from the pulpit.) Most preachers refuse to touch any controversial topics for fear of losing their position, and our moral footing has collapsed. The teachers of God's Word are supposed to be one of the "two prophets which are the two olive trees and the two lampstands that stand before the Lord of all the earth." (Revelation 11:4) They are supposed to bring healing and truth to the world, but on the most critical issues, they have not. Why not? Because they love money and prestige like Balaam did.

For someone to be a true messenger of the LORD, they must speak the LORD'S Word and not be under anyone else's control. They must not worry about what others might think or say or how much money they might gain or lose. That includes influence from government and secret societies and liability insurance that have no place in God's House. That's why we have freedom of religion which is freedom to speak the truth of God's Word. The gifts and callings of the LORD are a great honor and blessing, and should not be relinquished for anyone or anything for any reason.

There are some who have stood against the cabal powers and have lost their incomes and even their freedom and their lives. They have courageously fulfilled their duty as a messenger of the LORD. There are others who have bent the knee to the powers that be, and that's why the Church is in the shape it's in.

The Church is not a corporation.

The Church is not a club.

The Church is not a motivational kickstart to the week.

The Church is not a Mason-controlled organization.

The Church is the gathering of God's people.

No wonder the Bible says that in the End Times people will wander from border to border, to and fro searching for the Word and find none.

AMOS 8

12 "People will stagger from sea to sea
and wander from border to border
searching for the word of the Lord,
but they will not find it."

In case you think I'm being too hard on Balaam, this is what Peter said about Balaam and his type.

2nd PETER 2

14 "They commit adultery with their eyes, and their desire for sin is never satisfied. They lure unstable people into sin, and they are well trained in greed. They live under God's curse.

15 They have wandered off the right road and followed the footsteps of Balaam son of Beor, who loved to earn money by doing wrong.

16 But Balaam was stopped from his mad course when his donkey rebuked him with a human voice.

17 These people are as useless as dried-up springs or as mist blown away by the wind. They are doomed to blackest darkness.

18 They brag about themselves with empty, foolish boasting. With an appeal to twisted sexual desires, they lure back into sin those who have barely escaped from a lifestyle of deception.

19 They promise freedom, but they themselves are slaves of sin and corruption. For you are a slave to whatever controls you."

And would you look at this? In Jude 1:11 the Lord calls out Balaam for being a false prophet. You can't tell me it's a coincidence that it's 111! As in "111" which symbolizes "The Great Awakening" when the LORD said there would be false prophets who would work for money and not for the glory of God. Plus you can't tell me it's a coincidence that Prophet and Profit sound the same! Being a "prophet" for "profit" is rampant!

JUDE 1

11 "What sorrow awaits them! For they follow in the footsteps of Cain, who killed his brother. Like Balaam, they deceive people for money. And like Korah, they perish in their rebellion."

It is a very dangerous thing to take the name of the LORD in vain. What that means is to take the name of the LORD as if you are going to speak on His behalf, and then to fail to tell the people the truth! Intentionally or unintentionally. That is extremely dangerous territory.

EXODUS 20 NKJV

7 "You shall not take the name of the LORD your God in vain, for the LORD will not hold him guiltless who takes His name in vain."

Now, back to the story of Balaam and his false prophet ways.

The LORD said Balaam could go with the Moabites...BUT NOT TO CURSE HIS PEOPLE! Balaam was so excited! Off he went with the Moabites on his cursed business trip. He figured he could somehow negotiate a deal and end up with a big sack of money. The LORD knew exactly what Balaam was thinking. I imagine the whole trip Balaam was conniving how he could work this out so he didn't get in trouble God, but he could also please the Moabites and ride home with pockets full of gold. Balaam was not at all interested in the glory of God or the good of God's people. Balaam was a lousy stinking sell-out prophet.

It turned out that Balaam had one thing going for him. Balaam had a great donkey. The good little donkey was dutifully carrying Balaam's sorry behind to Moab, until at one point the donkey bolted off the path. What the donkey saw...that the Prophet Balaam did not see, was the Angel of the LORD in the path! Balaam was so angry he beat his donkey. Poor little donkey got a beating for saving sorry old Balaam's behind from the Angel!

The Angel of the LORD appeared again a little farther down the path where the path narrowed. To avoid the Angel and another beating, the good little donkey tried to squeeze through, but Balaam's foot got crushed. The poor little donkey got **another** beating!

I'm sure these emissaries thought Balaam was as crazy as they come. First he was not a good donkey driver. And second he had quite a temper for a "man of God!"

But Balaam could not see what the donkey could see. The donkey could literally see the Angel of the LORD. So now we know for sure from the Bible that animals are smarter than some people!

For a third time the little donkey saw the Angel of the LORD standing in middle of the path. There was no way for the donkey to go forward. So the good donkey just sat down and he took yet another beating from Balaam!

And guess what the Lord did! He gave Balaam's donkey the ability to speak! This is what the donkey said!

NUMBERS 22

28 *"Then the Lord gave the donkey the ability to speak. What have I done to you that deserves your beating me three times?" it asked Balaam.*

29 *"You have made me look like a fool!" Balaam shouted. "If I had a sword with me, I would kill you!""*

I think we would all agree that Balaam looked like a fool and it had nothing to do with the donkey! Which is typically the way it works. Usually people look like a fool because they are a fool, and it's their own fault. And not the fault of the others they try to blame.

Imagine this picture of Balaam and the donkey talking and reasoning in the path with the Moabite emissaries all watching. That must've been quite the sight! The Bible doesn't tell us if the emissaries could understand what the donkey was saying. I have a feeling they could only hear Balaam's side of the conversation. Yes he really did look like a fool! Here's what the donkey said next!

NUMBERS 22

30 "But I am the same donkey you have ridden all your life," the donkey answered. "Have I ever done anything like this before?" "No," Balaam admitted."

What a good donkey. He was just doing his job like he always did! He knew he was a good donkey and that he didn't deserve a beating. Balaam had to admit that it was true. He always had been a good donkey.

Then finally, Balaam saw the Angel of the LORD and he knew he was in big trouble!

NUMBERS 22

31 "Then the LORD opened Balaam's eyes, and he saw the Angel of the LORD standing in the roadway with a drawn sword in his hand. Balaam bowed his head and fell face down on the ground before him.

*32 "Why did you beat your donkey those three times?" the Angel of the LORD demanded. "Look, I have come to block your way because **you are stubbornly resisting me**. 33 Three times the donkey saw me and shied away; otherwise, I would certainly have killed you by now and spared the donkey."*

34 Then Balaam confessed to the Angel of the LORD, "I have sinned. I didn't realize you were standing in the road to block my way. I will return home if you are against my going."

35 But the Angel of the LORD told Balaam, "Go with these men, but say only what I tell you to say." So Balaam went on with Balak's officials."

The Lord knew exactly what Balaam was thinking. He was trying to finagle some way to have his cake and eat it too. Balaam was trying to find some way to curse God's people and not get in trouble with God.

You cannot fool God.

Ever.

Balaam, of all people, doesn't strike me as someone who could outwit the Living God!

I love that the first thing the Angel of the LORD asked Balaam was why he beat his donkey three times! The LORD sees EVERYTHING!!! And he cares for donkeys too! Then the Angel of the LORD said He was standing in the path because Balaam was stubbornly resisting Him. And that the donkey had saved his life! Three times!

I wonder if Balaam went and kissed his little donkey and hugged his neck. He should have. But I bet that self-centered, ungrateful wretch didn't! The LORD was reminding Balaam that He was watching. Balaam was commanded to go to this meeting with Balak, but to be very careful not to curse God's people. We are all living in very interesting times and we attend very interesting meetings where we are representing the LORD. Let it always be that we speak on His behalf and speak only His words. Lord speak through us and have us say only Your words at all times.

The Moabite emissaries didn't know what in the world was going on! They had no idea they were right smack dab in the middle of a Bible story that people would read for thousands of years.

And a funny one at that!

Balak, the Moabite king, was so excited to see Balaam arrive to curse the Israelites!

Balak was in for a big surprise.

NUMBERS 22

37 "Didn't I send you an urgent invitation? Why didn't you come right away?" Balak asked Balaam. "Didn't you believe me when I said I would reward you richly?"

38 Balaam replied, "Look, now I have come, but I have no power to say whatever I want. I will speak only the message that God puts in my mouth."

It appears that Balaam got the message loud and clear (5:5) from the Angel of the LORD. "Don't even think about cursing God's people." Balaam was between a rock and a hard spot. The rock was the LORD. And the hard spot was the LORD. He didn't have an inch of wiggle room. He had to do what the LORD said and that was all there was to it. But the Bible clearly says that Balaam was really only interested in the cash.

This is what happened. Balaam ended up causing the people who worshipped Baal to actually have a worship service to the LORD! That's hilarious! Balaam had them set up seven altars and sacrifice seven rams and seven bulls. Again with the 777!

Anybody seeing a pattern?

The Moabites did not want to hold a worship service to the LORD but they agreed because they thought they would get a curse for God's people out of it.

Then Balaam went to speak to the LORD.

NUMBERS 23

7 "This was the message Balaam delivered:

"Balak summoned me to come from Aram;

the king of Moab brought me from the eastern hills.

'Come,' he said, 'curse Jacob for me!

Come and announce Israel's doom.'

8 But how can I curse those

whom God has not cursed?

How can I condemn those whom

the Lord has not condemned?
9 I see them from the cliff tops;
I watch them from the hills.
I see a people who live by themselves,
set apart from other nations.
10 Who can count Jacob's descendants,
as numerous as dust?
Who can count even a fourth of Israel's people?
Let me die like the righteous;
let my life end like theirs."

Balaam couldn't do it. He wanted the money. He really did. He wanted to speak something to load up his pockets. He just couldn't. The words would **not** come out of his mouth!

I can just see the look on Balaam's face. He shrugged his shoulders as if to say, "I have no control over what is coming out of my mouth."

Balaam's eyes told King Balak he wanted to proclaim a curse. But Balaam's mouth couldn't do it! Many preachers in our day have taken the filthy lucre and are willing to say and do anything they are told. The NWO Cabal knows that people trust "men of the cloth" so they are a tremendous asset! The Agenda 21 plans include using those whom the people trust, to guide them into complete enslavement. <u>But the LORD will not allow that</u>.

LORD do not allow the modern-day preachers to curse Your people and help the Cabal to enslave them. Do not allow any deception to come out of their mouths. In Jesus' name.

Balak, the Moabite King, wanted to try again to see if Balaam could curse the Israelites. He needed a curse and he was going to get one!

This time they were looking out over all the Israelites from

Mount Pisgah. Balaam had them do the same thing all over again. Build seven altars and sacrifice seven rams and seven bulls.

Balaam went to speak with the LORD and received this message:

NUMBERS 23

18 "This was the message Balaam delivered:

"Rise up, Balak, and listen! Hear me, son of Zippor.

19 God is not a man, so he does not lie.

He is not human, so he does not change his mind.

Has he ever spoken and failed to act?

Has he ever promised and not carried it through?

20 Listen, I received a command to bless;

God has blessed, and I cannot reverse it!

21 No misfortune is in his plan for Jacob;

no trouble is in store for Israel.

For the Lord their God is with them;

he has been proclaimed their king.

22 God brought them out of Egypt;

for them he is as strong as a wild ox.

23 No curse can touch Jacob;

no magic has any power against Israel.

For now it will be said of Jacob,

'What wonders God has done for Israel!'

24 These people rise up like a lioness,

like a majestic lion rousing itself.

They refuse to rest until they have feasted on prey,

drinking the blood of the slaughtered!""

I can just see Balak, king of the Moabites, doing a face palm! He couldn't believe that God's people had been blessed and the

Moabites had been cursed AGAIN! This was not what he had in mind at all!

NUMBERS 23

25"Then Balak said to Balaam, "Fine, but if you won't curse them, at least don't bless them!"

26 But Balaam replied to Balak, "Didn't I tell you that I can do only what the Lord tells me?""

It seems that Balaam literally had no control over what was coming out of his mouth. <u>The LORD would not let curses on His people come out of Balaam's mouth.</u>

But Balak wanted to give it one more try. I think Balak thought Balaam wanted that money as bad as he wanted that curse on the Israelites. So this time they headed to Mount Peor.

The Bible says that Balaam did not resort to **divination**…like magic charms to call on the LORD.

Balaam knew the LORD was going to bless Israel and the Spirit of GOD came upon him and this is the message he delivered:

NUMBERS 24

3b "This is the message of Balaam son of Beor,

the message of the man whose eyes see clearly,

4 the message of one who hears the words of God,

who sees a vision from the Almighty,

who bows down with eyes wide open:

5 How beautiful are your tents, O Jacob;

how lovely are your homes, O Israel!

6 They spread before me like palm groves,

like gardens by the riverside.

They are like tall trees planted by the Lord,

like cedars beside the waters.

7 Water will flow from their buckets;

their offspring have all they need.

Their king will be greater than Agag;

their kingdom will be exalted.

8 God brought them out of Egypt;

for them he is as strong as a wild ox.

He devours all the nations that oppose him,

breaking their bones in pieces,

shooting them with arrows.

9 Like a lion, Israel crouches and lies down;

like a lioness, who dares to arouse her?

Blessed is everyone who blesses you,

O Israel, and cursed is everyone who curses you."

That was the last straw for Balak, the Moabite king!

NUMBERS 24

10 "King Balak flew into a rage against Balaam.

He angrily clapped his hands and shouted,

"I called you to curse my enemies!

Instead, you have blessed them three times.

11 Now get out of here! Go back home!

I promised to reward you richly,

but the Lord has kept you from your reward."

Well, Balaam didn't care that King Balak was having a fit! And since Balak said he wouldn't pay Balaam a nickel, Balaam let her rip! Balaam was filled with the Spirit of the Lord and he gave King Balak another piece of the LORD'S mind. This prophecy is about the complete annihilation of those who are possessed by demons. This prophecy is what we are witnessing being fulfilled!

NUMBERS 24

15 "This is the message Balaam delivered:

"This is the message of Balaam son of Beor,

the message of the man whose eyes see clearly,

16 the message of one who hears the words of God,

who has knowledge from the Most High,

who sees a vision from the Almighty,

who bows down with eyes wide open:

17 I see him, but not here and now.

*I perceive him, but **far in the distant future.***

A star will rise from Jacob;

a scepter will emerge from Israel.

It will <u>crush the heads of Moab's people</u>,

cracking the skulls of the people of Sheth.

<u>18 Edom will be taken over</u>,

and <u>Seir, its enemy, will be conquered</u>,

while Israel marches on in triumph.

19 A ruler will rise in Jacob

who will destroy the survivors of Ir."

20 Then Balaam looked over

toward the people of Amalek

and delivered this message:

"Amalek was the greatest of nations,

but its destiny is destruction!"

21 Then he looked over toward the Kenites

and delivered this message:

"Your home is secure; your nest is set in the rocks.

22 But the Kenites will be destroyed

when Assyria takes you captive."
23 "Balaam concluded his messages by saying:
"Alas, who can survive unless God has willed it?"
24 Ships will come from the coasts of Cyprus;
they will oppress Assyria and afflict Eber,
but they, too, will be utterly destroyed.""

Balaam went on a rant like you've never heard before! He went scorched earth on those heathen demon worshipers! He foretold their utter destruction from the face of the earth. That time that Balaam foresaw "far in the distant future" is **now**. We are witnessing the "**scepter emerging from Israel!**" That is Christ ruling the earth, and us along with Him! Nothing can stop what is coming because THIS IS BIBLICAL!

Of course, Balaam didn't get a nickel for all his trouble! He didn't even get travel expenses. I bet Balaam had to file bankruptcy and close down his prophet profiteering business!

LORD may it be in our day that we have true ministers of Your Word who speak the truth and don't care what anybody says except for You!

How's THAT for a Bible story?

What is the main takeaway from this historical account of Balaam?

The LORD has destined us for blessing.

He will not allow the enemy to triumph over us.

The LORD will not allow the satanic curses to fall on us.

No weapon formed against us will prosper.

Nothing can separate us from the love of God which is in Christ Jesus our LORD. Neither death, nor life, nor angels, nor demons, nor things in heaven, nor hell...not even false preachers.

Nothing can separate us from the love of God in Christ Jesus.

They can try and try and try again.
All the plans to destroy God's people will fail.

The Lord has destined us for victory.

And nothing can stop what is coming!

12 JEHOSHAPHAT - GET YOUR TAMBOURINE

I refuse to fear-monger. It might get clicks. But the Freedom Force Battalion is about faith. Not fear. We know the LORD will give us the victory and that keeps us strong for the battle. As 17 says, "Be careful who you follow." People tell me they've had it up to here with the fear-mongering from other sites and they prefer to advance the fight of faith, not fear. We know the enemy is fierce. We know they don't fight fair. But we know the LORD's promises are true. And, that as we pray and praise the LORD, we will be victorious! That's what Jehoshaphat knew too!

Jehoshaphat was the King of Israel when they were just getting settled in the land of Canaan. There were still fierce demon-worshiping enemies on all sides. But the Israelites knew the LORD had seen them miraculously walk across the Red Sea, and through the Jordan, and they saw the Walls of Jericho come tumblin' down, so they trusted the LORD would save them from their enemies. Well, what a coincidence! We believe the LORD will save us from **our** enemies too! This is what happened with King Jehoshaphat, and how they won the victory:

2nd CHRONICLES 20

1 "After this, the armies of the Moabites, Ammonites, and some of the Meunites declared war on Jehoshaphat. 2 Messengers came and told Jehoshaphat, "A vast army from Edom is marching against you from beyond the Dead Sea. They are already at Hazazon-tamar." (This was another name for En-gedi.)"

Remember Edomites were Esau's descendants. Remember, Esau was the evil twin brother of Jacob, whose name was changed to Israel. The Edomites are just like the New World Order. They aren't satisfied unless they are causing trouble, stealing, killing, and destroying. Notice they came from "beyond the Dead Sea." The Dead Sea symbolizes death. Nothing can live in the Dead Sea because of its high salt content. And nothing good lives long with these creeps. Death and destruction are always in their paths. Jehoshaphat knew all about them. They were straight out of Central Casting for horror movies. And Jehoshaphat was terrified. But he did what we do. He begged the LORD for guidance, and fasted.

2nd CHRONICLES 20

3 *"Jehoshaphat was terrified by this news and begged the LORD for guidance. He also ordered everyone in Judah to begin fasting.*

4 So people from all the towns of Judah came to Jerusalem to seek the LORD's help. 5 Jehoshaphat stood before the community of Judah and Jerusalem in front of the new courtyard at the Temple of the LORD.

6 He prayed, "O LORD, God of our ancestors,

you alone are the God who is in heaven.

You are ruler of all the kingdoms of the earth.

You are powerful and mighty;

no one can stand against you!

7 O our God, did you not drive out

 those who lived in this land

when your people Israel arrived?

And did you not give this land forever

to the descendants of your friend Abraham?

8 Your people settled here and

built this Temple to honor your name.

9 They said, 'Whenever we are faced with any calamity

such as war, plague, or famine,

we can come to stand in your presence

before this Temple where your name is honored.

We can cry out to you to save us,

and you will hear us and rescue us.'"

We know the promises of the LORD and when we are faced with calamity, we go to the LORD and we know He will hear us and rescue us. Throughout the ups and downs and twists and turns of this Battle of Armageddon, this confidence has kept us strong and at peace. Thank You LORD for our faith that gives us the victory!

2nd CHRONICLES 20

10 "And now see what the armies of Ammon,

Moab, and Mount Seir are doing.

You would not let our ancestors

invade those nations when Israel left Egypt,

so they went around them and did not destroy them.

11 Now see how they reward us!

For they have come to throw us out of your land,

which you gave us as an inheritance.

12 O our God, won't you stop them?

We are powerless against this

mighty army that is about to attack us.

We do not know what to do,

but we are looking to you for help."

For the LORD'S own reasons He did not allow these enemies to be destroyed before. Much like the New World Order. But this historical account of Jehoshaphat is about how the LORD destroyed these enemies when the time came, just like we are witnessing happening to the NWO criminal mafia cabal!

2ⁿᵈ CHRONICLES 20

13 "As all the men of Judah stood before the LORD with their little ones, wives, and children,

14 the Spirit of the LORD came upon one of the men standing there. His name was Jahaziel son of Zechariah, son of Benaiah, son of Jeiel, son of Mattaniah, a Levite who was a descendant of Asaph.

15 He said, "Listen, all you
people of Judah and Jerusalem!
Listen, King Jehoshaphat!
This is what the LORD says: Do not be afraid!
Don't be discouraged by this mighty army,
for the battle is not yours, but God's."

I love this man of faith, Jahaziel! He was inspired by the LORD to say just exactly what the people needed to hear at that moment! His faith turned the Israelite's fear into faith too! Jahaziel was a Levite, and his tribe was responsible for the worship of the LORD. He was a descendant of Asaph who wrote several of the psalms the people sang in worship! Search "Psalm of Asaph" in *BibleGateway.com* and you will see the psalms Asaph wrote. But most importantly, those songs of inspiration lept off the page and straight into the heart of his grandson, and then into the hearts of the Israelites. Let's remember that, Patriots! Do not be discouraged by any mighty army, for the battle is not yours, but God's! Wait until you hear how they won the victory!

2ⁿᵈ CHRONICLES 20

16 "Tomorrow, march out against them. You will find them coming up through the ascent of Ziz at the end of the valley that opens into the wilderness of Jeruel.

17 But you will not even need to fight. Take your positions; then stand still and watch the LORD's victory. He is with you, O people of Judah and Jerusalem. Do not be afraid or discouraged. Go out against them tomorrow, for the LORD is with you!"

These are just like our orders.

March out against them.

Step out in faith.

You will not even need to fight.

Just like in our Battle of Armageddon.

We aren't fighting in regular warfare.

We are fighting with truth!

Stand still and watch the LORD'S victory.

Do not be afraid or discouraged.

The LORD is with us!

What a relief!

Our victory is sure!

2nd CHRONICLES 20

18 "Then King Jehoshaphat bowed low

with his face to the ground.

And all the people of Judah and

Jerusalem did the same, worshiping the LORD.

19 Then the Levites from the clans of

Kohath and Korah stood to praise the LORD,

the God of Israel, with a very loud shout.

20 Early the next morning the army of Judah

went out into the wilderness of Tekoa.

On the way Jehoshaphat stopped and said,

"Listen to me, all you people of Judah and Jerusalem!

Believe in the LORD your God,

and you will be able to stand firm.

Believe in his prophets, and you will succeed."

How will we be able to stand firm and succeed?

Believe the LORD our God.
Simple.

2nd CHRONICLES 20

21 "After consulting the people,
the king appointed singers
to walk ahead of the army,
singing to the LORD and praising him
for his holy splendor.
This is what they sang:
"Give thanks to the LORD;
his faithful love endures forever!"
22 At the very moment they began
to sing and give praise,
the LORD caused the armies of
Ammon, Moab, and Mount Seir
to start fighting among themselves.
23 The armies of Moab and Ammon
turned against their allies from Mount Seir
and killed every one of them.
After they had destroyed the army of Seir,
they began attacking each other.
24 So when the army of Judah arrived
at the lookout point in the wilderness,
all they saw were dead bodies
lying on the ground as far as they could see.
Not a single one of the enemy had escaped."

Let's continually have this song in our hearts!
"Give thanks to the LORD;

his faithful love endures forever!"

It surely does.

He is with us now, just as He was with our ancestors!

At the very moment they began to sing and give praise, the LORD caused their enemies to destroy each other!

So let's keeping praising and singing everybody!

Praise Him for the victory and His promises.. for all He has done and all He has promised to do. He is worthy. And it's good for us too! Sing songs! Sing hymns! Make melody in your heart! Keep a "Thankful List" on your fridge and it will bless your entire home to win the victory!

Jehoshaphat's "battle" is much like the Battle of Gideon! Remember? The enemies destroyed each other! God's people just stood still and watched the LORD's win for them! The only job was carrying home all the plunder!

2nd CHRONICLES 20

25 "King Jehoshaphat and his men
went out to gather the plunder.
They found vast amounts of
equipment, clothing, and other valuables—
more than they could carry.
There was so much plunder
that it took them three days
just to collect it all!
26 On the fourth day they
gathered in the Valley of Blessing,
which got its name that day because
the people praised and thanked the LORD there.
It is still called the Valley of Blessing today."

The entire earth will be the Valley of Blessing.

Everyone will receive back the plunder that has been stolen from them, and then some! And everyone will praise the LORD and thank Him, which is the biggest blessing of all!

Everyone will know the LORD from the least to the greatest! The earth will be filled with the glory of the LORD, as the waters fill the sea!

2nd CHRONICLES 20

27 "Then all the men returned to Jerusalem,
with Jehoshaphat leading them,
overjoyed that the LORD had given
them victory over their enemies.
28 They marched into Jerusalem to
the music of harps, lyres, and trumpets,
and they proceeded to the Temple of the LORD.
29 When all the surrounding kingdoms heard that
the LORD himself had fought against
the enemies of Israel, the fear of God came over them.
30 So Jehoshaphat's kingdom was at peace,
for his God had given him rest on every side."

Once we cast our enemies into the abyss, we will have peace on earth, good will toward men. We will have rest on every side. The LORD said we will look for our enemies and we will not be able to find them. Not only will we not find our enemies, like Bill Gates, we won't find any enemies at all! We won't find anything to harm us on all of God's holy mountain. And as the LORD promised in Revelation 20, there will be no more deception for 1,000 years!

That's something to sing about!

Now, where did I put my tambourine?!

13 ELIJAH - DESTROYING THE PROPHETS OF BAAL

Of all the historical accounts recorded in the Bible, the one about the showdown between Elijah and the prophets of Baal makes it absolutely clear that we are fulfilling all these Bible stories in our current day. I've probably talked about this historical account more than any other. It was actually one of the first Bible stories I ever told on my original YouTube channel way back in April 2018. My channel was banned, but I think I titled the video something like, "Our Military Destroys the Epstein Island Prophets of Baal." Come to think of it, maybe that was one of the reasons my channel was banned!

Somehow that video went viral even though I was just sitting by rose bush just telling the Bible story. Before that, my videos only had a few hundred views. Someone in the comment section said a military officer had told the soldiers to watch my video so they could understand how they were destroying Baal worship as they cleaned out Epstein Island! WOW! Most had likely never heard the story. But that military officer knew the extraordinary Biblical significance of what they were doing. Epstein Island was one of the strongholds of Baal worship, and our amazing military was demolishing it! That's what this story of Elijah is all about.

The Prophet Elijah lived during the reign of evil King Ahab of the northern tribes of Israel. Ahab was married to evil Queen Jezebel. Jezebel had brought to Israel her evil practice of worshiping demons. She had 450 prophets of Baal and 400 prophets of Asherah that she paid for their evil services.

Now you know why no one names their child Jezebel. Make no

mistake. Jezebel received the judgment she was so deserving of...as our LORD Jesus said:

MARK 9 NKJV

48 "their worm does not die and the fire is not quenched."

The unspeakable evil Jezebel wrought in Israel was well-deserving of the eternal wrath of God. But Elijah stood up against Ahab and Jezebel. Most of the prophets had either been killed or were in hiding because of evil Ahab's and Jezebel's reign of terror in the land. Obadiah hid away 100 prophets and provided for them, because Ahab and Jezebel hunted them down.

1st KINGS 18

4 "Once when Jezebel had tried to kill all the Lord's prophets, Obadiah had hidden 100 of them in two caves. He put fifty prophets in each cave and supplied them with food and water."

By the grace of God, Elijah escaped their hit squads. Elijah asked the LORD what he could do to stop the satanic sacrifices to Baal, and the LORD told Elijah to pray for the rain to stop. And it did. There was no rain for three and a half years. (3½ years = 42 months = 1260 days = Time, Times, and Half a Time= Jupiter/ Melchizedek loop. See *"End Times and 1000 Years of Peace."*) The Bible says this about Elijah:

JAMES 5

16 "The earnest prayer of a righteous person has great power and produces wonderful results. 17 Elijah was as human as we are, and yet when he prayed earnestly that no rain would fall, none fell for three and a half years!"

Elijah doesn't seem like an "ordinary" man to me. LORD give us courage like Elijah. Three and a half years without rain would probably get everyone's attention. Eventually Jezebel and Ahab felt the consequences of the drought, and they were piping hot angry at Elijah. They called him the "Troubler of Israel." How ironic. THEY were the troublers of Israel, not Elijah. Typical. Good old projection. They blame the righteous for the very evil they do. Elijah was not shy to speak the truth right to Ahab's face.

1ˢᵗ KINGS 18

18 "I have made no trouble for Israel," Elijah replied. "You and your family are the troublemakers, for you have refused to obey the commands of the Lord and have worshiped the images of Baal instead. 19 Now summon all Israel to join me at Mount Carmel, along with the 450 prophets of Baal and the 400 prophets of Asherah who are supported by Jezebel."

Ahab and Jezebel knew they were not going to get any rain until Elijah asked the LORD to open the sky. And now that Elijah had challenged them to a showdown on Mount Carmel, the gig was up. All of Israel was buzzing with the news! It was the Prophet Super Bowl and everyone was going to be there! Ahab and Jezebel had to accept the challenge. For some odd reason Jezebel didn't go to the Super Bowl showdown between Elijah and her false prophets. More about why later. Here is the view of the expansive Jezreel Valley from Mount Carmel. This area is located in central Israel.

Imagine everyone in Israel gathered to see what would happen! Isn't that where we are as humanity right now? We're all watching to see who will be victorious: the satanic New World Order or Trump along with the white hats and Patriots. This is the ultimate showdown of good versus evil. Elijah wasn't worried one bit. He actually thought it was funny to see the Baal worshipers' futile attempt to compete against the true and living God. I think all of us will be a lot happier if we do the same. Laugh at these creeps as they flail about and fight and experience their last gasps to maintain power.

This is how the showdown worked. Both the prophets of Baal and Elijah set up an altar of stones with wood on top. On the altar, each placed a sacrificial bull, and then they called upon their God to light the sacrifice on fire. Only the true God would set fire to the sacrifice.

The LORD commanded for sacrifices to be offered, as a way for the people to show their repentance and need of forgiveness. The LORD would respond that He received their offering and that their sins were forgiven, by lighting the sacrifice on fire.

Of course, the Baal worshipers always performed a counterfeit ceremony. Under normal circumstances, their temple was arranged so someone underneath the altar would light the fire and the people were fooled into thinking Baal lit it. The ultimate fake news.

I'm not going to describe the evil sacrifices, like what occurred at Epstein Island. Search Bohemian Grove and the Black Forest and other places around the world where the NWO "elite" have performed hideous and horrifying satanic sacrifices. Those who participated were recorded on video so everyone was controlled and would never break their vows to the New World Order. Yes. That's how the system of evil has worked...like a charm. Most of the leaders in the top positions are the most guilty. Rest assured, this is the Day when this terrifying evil will stop. White hats have all the evidence of these atrocities, and those who did this evil will be brought to justice for their crimes against humanity. That sounds outrageous, and it is, but there is undeniable evidence that this is true. That is what the WikiLeaks were about, as well as Epstein Island, along with the Jeffrey Epstein and the Ghislaine Maxwell trial and Ghislaine's famous list of "customers" that has never been revealed...yet. There is plenty of undeniable evidence, which is readily available on alternative websites, despite the fact that the main social media channels have censored this information and ban those who share it.)

Humanity is like all those people on Mount Carmel, watching the showdown between Elijah and the prophets of Baal. It was quite the show. Elijah told the prophets of Baal they could go first. It's like President Trump letting the Deep State do their worst to him, until they have completely expended their fake news ammo. That's exactly what happened with the prophets of Baal. The prophets set up the altar with the stones and the wood and the sacrificial bull. Then they began to perform their dance routine, calling on Baal to light the sacrifice. But nothing happened.

So they danced around, and then danced more, and then dance some more, yelling louder to Baal to light the sacrifice. No one could understand why it wasn't working this time! But Elijah knew. It was because Jezebel's minion was not able to stand underneath the altar to light the fire as they always did in the Baal temple! This was probably why Jezebel didn't come to the showdown. This did not deter the prophets of Baal. They kept dancing around and even started cutting themselves to get Baal's attention. It was quite a show. And I bet it wasn't PG-13 either. Imagine "drag events" times 1,000.

They were just like these New World Order fools who are gyrating all over the media and politics, trying to hide the lies to maintain their power. They look like a bunch of fools to us, because we know the truth, just like Elijah did! Elijah was enjoying the show! He started making fun of them, telling them to yell louder because Baal might be taking a nap! Or maybe Baal had gone to the bathroom! The more you make fun of them, the madder they get, and the happier you will be! That's what President Trump has been doing, along with Elon Musk and Steve Bannon, Kid Rock and Ted Nugent, and Tucker Carlson and 17, of course! Patriots, let's keep calling out the NWO fools' stupidity every day!!

Finally, these prophets of Baal were exhausted. They couldn't dance around and cut themselves any more.

They were spent.

Worn out.

Kaput!

They finally gave up.

What does that tell us about satan's power?

He has zero power.

The only power satan has is the power to work through people who surrender their power to him!

Finally...it was Elijah's turn. He built up the altar of the LORD that had been broken down. He used 12 stones representing the 12 tribes of Israel. (These are the 12 families of God who are destined to lead the world in righteousness.) Elijah was using those 12 stones to remind the brainwashed fools that they had a bigger destiny than to worship demons! They were from the chosen family of Israel! Elijah was trying to help them break the hypnotic spell that duped them into thinking they were worshiping God, when they were really worshiping Baal!

Elijah dug a trench around the altar. Then Elijah placed the sacrifice on the altar and soaked the altar and the sacrifice with water. Soaked it with water?!! That wasn't part of the usual ceremony! Why would Elijah do that? He even poured water all over the altar and the sacrifice a second time. And then he poured water all over the altar and the sacrifice a third time. The water even filled the trench! He was showing the people that what they were about to witness was not a magician's trick. What they were about to witness would be a literal miracle from the LORD. The lighting of the altar would be from the LORD and not from any little man with a torch underneath the altar. Elijah was showing the people undeniable evidence that the LORD is the True and Living God.

I don't know what is going to happen at this worldwide showdown between good and evil, but at some point, everyone will know that the LORD is the True and Living God. Everyone will know that all of this deception and confusion and mayhem has just been evil tricks from those who follow demons.

The Minor Prophets say over and over that the demon worshipers will be exposed and cast out, and the LORD Himself will be King. That fact won't be left for anyone to wonder. It will be clear that this victory for humanity was the LORD'S doing. I'm not sure exactly how that's going to happen, but it will be marvelous! And justice will be everywhere! True law and order. Justice will be meted out on the top leaders in every area - government and military and business and medical. Peace will settle worldwide.

In Elijah's showdown with the Baal worshipers, Elijah stood before all the people and they were just staring at him. Was Elijah going to dance around? Was he going to cut himself? Would he say some strange cantation?

1st KINGS 18

36 "At the usual time for offering the evening sacrifice, Elijah the prophet walked up to the altar and prayed, "O Lord, God of Abraham, Isaac, and Jacob, prove today that you are God in Israel and that I am your servant. Prove that I have done all this at your command. 37 O Lord, answer me! Answer me so these people will know that you, O Lord, are God and that you have brought them back to yourself.

38 Immediately *the fire of the LORD flashed down from heaven and burned up the young bull, the wood, the stones, and the dust. It even licked up all the water in the trench! 39 And when all the people saw it, they fell face down on the ground and cried out, "The LORD—He is God! Yes, the LORD is God!"*

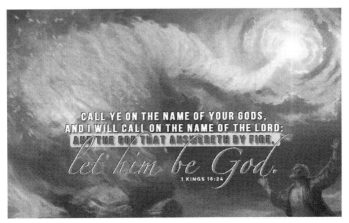

WOW!! Like a Lighting Bolt!!

The LORD God answered!

The fire from the LORD licked up the sacrifice,

evaporated the wood on the altar,

vaporized the stones on the altar,

and even drank up every drop of water in the trench!

Honestly, if the LORD had not held back, He would have consumed all the people too!

It's so easy for the LORD to reveal His great power. Elijah prayed one simple short prayer, and the LORD answered in the most powerful, undeniable, spectacular way.

The people knew immediately they had been deceived into following the prophets of Baal. There was no question in their minds that they had been completely duped. They fell on their faces and cried, "The LORD is God!" How could we have been so deceived?

Our family and friends will soon ask themselves that same question, "How could we have been so deceived?" We will need to help them understand the truth, and understand that we have ALL been tricked.

Did you catch this part of Elijah's prayer?

> 37 "O Lord, Answer me so these people will know that you, O Lord, are God and that you have brought them back to yourself."

I love that Elijah wanted the people to know **that the LORD had brought them back to Himself.** Elijah knew the people would be filled with guilt and overwhelming regret for following those priests of Baal. They would need to know the LORD had forgiven them, and that He would help them to forgive themselves. They would need to know the LORD loved them and was rescuing them, not destroying them. The same applies to all the brainwashed masses in our day. The LORD loves us. He forgives us. He knows "they know not what they do." The LORD is rescuing us all. Did you hear that? He is RESCUING HUMANITY.

Can you just imagine the look of horror and despair on the faces of those false priests of Baal? We will soon see those looks on the faces of Fauci and Gates and Soros. The people will be filled with rage at them for lying and misleading them into such atrocities, and for all their crimes against humanity. Elijah commanded:

1st KINGS 18

40 *"Seize all the prophets of Baal. Don't let a single one escape!" So the people seized them all, and Elijah took them down to the Kishon Valley and killed them there."*

Here's an aerial map of Mt. Carmel with the Jezreel Valley an Kishon River below. That's were all the prophets of Baal and Asherah were executed.

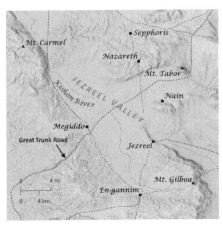

That's what you call a quick trial.

No fancy attorney to get the conviction overturned on a technicality.

No asinine rule that thwarts justice.

They were guilty.

They were executed.

All 450 prophets of Baal.

And all 400 prophets of Asherah.

Not one escaped.

End of story.

Maybe this was why Jezebel was a no-show.

The false prophets will be destroyed. Make no mistake about it. They know they will and that's why they are fighting so hard and foolishly exposing themselves with all these ridiculous and obvious lies. From the election fraud, to the Covid and the jab debacle, to the Omnibus theft and the money laundered through Ukraine, to the Hunter Biden "Laptop from Hell", to the border disaster. These demon worshipers know that the fate the prophets of Baal and Asherah received, is their fate.
They have no hope of escaping judgment.

To be frank, what happens on this earth is the least of it.

It will so be rewarding to see them paraded in open shame before all the world for their crimes against us...I'm talking about Fauci and Gates and Soros and Schwab and all the ones who committed demonic crimes against the world. They will soon meet the same fate as the prophets of Baal and Asherah.

Guess what happened next! There had been no rain for 3 1/2 years! Remember? Everyone was told to hurry home because the rains were coming!

Humanity has been in need of a good rain. A good soaking rain of blessings! Financial rain buckets of money! And buckets of health! Showers of restoration! A flood of peace! Get ready! The storm of God's fury is on them, but the showers of blessings are on us!

1st KINGS 18

41 "Then Elijah said to Ahab, "I hear a mighty rainstorm coming!"

42 So Ahab went to eat and drink. But Elijah climbed to the top of Mount Carmel and bowed low to the ground and prayed with his face between his knees.

43 Then he said to his servant, "Go and look out toward the sea." The servant went and looked, then returned to Elijah and said, "I didn't see anything." **Seven times** *Elijah told him to go and look.*

44 Finally the **seventh time,** *his servant told him, "I saw a little cloud about the size of a man's hand rising from the sea." Then Elijah shouted, "Hurry to Ahab and tell him, 'Climb into your chariot and go back home. If you don't hurry, the rain will stop you!'"*

45 And soon the sky was black with clouds.

A heavy wind brought a terrific rainstorm, and Ahab left quickly for Jezreel.

46 Then the LORD gave special strength to Elijah. He tucked his cloak into his belt and ran ahead of Ahab's chariot all the way to the entrance of Jezreel."

Notice that Elijah was praying and watching, sending his servant to see if the answer to his prayer had arrived. On the seventh time that he prayed, the LORD sent the answer. That's like the walls of Jericho coming down on the 7th day, on the 7th time around the walls. I bet we will see the 777 fulfilled at our Armageddon victory too. Let's keep praying and watching, Patriots!

Elijah was so filled with strength he ran faster than Ahab's chariot! In the Millennial Kingdom there will be nothing to hold back the rains of God's blessings on us as He pours out His Spirit on all flesh.

There will be plenty.

There will be health.

There will be peace.

There will be joy.

There will be showers of blessings and joy that no one can take away!

14 JOSIAH - WHEN THE RIGHTEOUS RULE

We are so very blessed to live in this day when all these evil satanic rituals will be torn down and stopped! We didn't even know these atrocities were happening literally right underneath our feet! But now that we know, nothing will stop our fight until the earth is purged of such evil demon worship.

This chapter is about a wonderful king who felt the very same way. The historical account of King Josiah is tucked into 2nd Kings Chapter 22, and he is rarely talked about. But in my opinion, he is one of the most memorable characters in the entire Bible. He ascended to the throne at the ripe age of eight years old. He tore down all the pagan altars throughout all of Israel. See what I mean by a memorable character?

King Josiah was very intentional about doing a good job as the King of Judah. But he did not have the written Word of God recorded in the Law of Moses. The written Word of God had been hidden intentionally by prior kings. And it seems that no one was allowed to teach the Word of God! Imagine that! No freedom of religion in Israel! Josiah was simply doing what was right in his mind to the best of his ability. But Josiah had a good heart, which we will soon discover.

One day King Josiah sent workers to restore God's temple. During the restoration process, the Law of Moses was discovered. They brought the book to King Josiah and they read it to him. Immediately, King Josiah realized they had been sinning against the LORD. He was sick with grief! He tore his clothes in torment! They hadn't done what they should have done. And they had done evil that they shouldn't have done! Imagine a society thinking child sacrifice was something God wanted! That sounds OUTRAGEOUS! But the Israelites were so brainwashed, they literally thought they were obeying God by sacrificing their children! See Micah Chapter 6:

MICAH 6

6 *"With what shall I come before the Lord,*
And bow myself before the High God?
Shall I come before Him with burnt offerings,
With calves a year old?
7 Will the Lord be pleased with thousands of rams,
Ten thousand rivers of oil?
*Shall **I give my firstborn for my transgression,***
***The fruit of my body for the sin of my soul**?"*

What? What were they thinking? They actually thought they should sacrifice their children to pay for their sins! It is so easy to judge the prior generations as being evil and foolish. But we have, in one generation, seen our society crumble due to the lack of the Word of God being proclaimed and justice being carried out. The degradation has sped up like a runaway train careening over a cliff! And that is happening in our day, when:

we know the LORD Jesus and have received forgiveness because He died for us,

and we have the Holy Spirit dwelling within us,

and we have the complete Word of God at our fingertips,

and we have the restraints set up in our Constitution!

And even still, look at the mess our world is in!

So let's not be quick to judge, because they could judge us right back!

Most societies go the way of their leaders. Here's the basic summary of 1st and 2nd Kings.
Good King – Good Society

Bad King – Bad Society
Bad King – Bad Society
Bad King – Bad Society
Good King – Good Society
Bad King – Bad Society
Bad King – Bad Society
Bad King – Bad Society
Bad King – Bad Society

See a pattern?

The history of most of the kings of Israel was that whether they knew the Law of Moses, or didn't know the Law of Moses, they did what they wanted to do anyway. But not Josiah! He was determined to follow the Law of Moses now that he had discovered it. He tore down all the Asherah poles and ground them to dust. He executed the priests of Baal on their own altars! And Josiah tore down all the pagan altars everywhere he could find them all throughout Israel. He got rid of the psychics and the household gods and every other detestable practice. Go Josiah!

Josiah had all the people gather together and he read to them what the Law of Moses said, and how the LORD was actually angry at them for sacrificing their children to Molech.

Imagine their shock.

Imagine their regret.

They realized they had been horribly misled.

This realization will soon dawn on all of humanity. Everyone will realize they have been deceived and will be forced to come to grips with the terrible choices they made while under the New World Order's spell. There will be mourning and regret as described in Zechariah 12.

ZECHARIAH 12

10 "Then I will pour out a spirit of grace and prayer on the family of David and on the people of Jerusalem. They will look on me whom they have pierced and mourn for him as for an only son. They will grieve bitterly for him as for a firstborn son who has died.

11 The sorrow and mourning in Jerusalem on that day will be like the great mourning for Hadad-rimmon in the valley of Megiddo.

12 "All Israel will mourn, each clan by itself, and with the husbands separate from their wives. The clan of David will mourn alone, as will the clan of Nathan,

13 the clan of Levi, and the clan of Shimei.

14 Each of the surviving clans from Judah will mourn separately, and with the husbands separate from their wives."

The mourning for Hadad-rimmon in the valley of Megiddo in Zechariah 12:11 refers to the mourning at the death of Great King Josiah. He was killed by Pharaoh Neco after reigning righteously for 31 years. The people were broken-hearted that their king who had brought so much peace and prosperity to the land, was gone. The demons were working through the power structure and no doubt had an evil hand in killing Josiah. The people's grief was not unwarranted. Pharaoh Neco installed Josiah's evil son, Jehoiakim, to rule and tax the people to pay tribute to Egypt. That is why the people were overcome with grief and there was great mourning throughout the nation.

Most Bible students agree that this mourning is apocalyptic and refers to the beginning of the Millennial Kingdom. That makes sense because we all mourned when we realized how horribly humanity has been tricked into doing evil, and abused by demons for literally thousands of years.

The deep regret will affect each one in a powerful and personal way. Each one of us will need to spend time in reconciliation with the LORD, privately. We are all in need of His forgiveness. We are all in need of His restoration. We will all need to give each other space and grace as we come to grips with what we have done, and what we have failed to do.

But we will not be grieving without hope. We know the love of Christ from the blood He shed for us on the cross, to forgive us and reconcile us. And, humanity's grief will be tempered with the realization that those days of evil and tyranny and deception are finally over!

Just like under King Josiah's leadership, all the people turned to the LORD and stopped worshiping demons! No more demon possession!

Absolutely amazing!

Look what can happen! The righteous in positions of authority can turn an entire nation back to the LORD and sanity! We are seeing this in our day, my friend!

There will be no more idol (demon) worship!

There will be no more Baal sacrifices!

There will be no more evil detestable practices!

This is the promise of the LORD and this is where humanity is headed! Not just in a little country called Israel in the Middle East, but over all the entire earth. This is the promise the LORD told us through the Minor Prophets.

HABAKKUK 2

14 "For as the waters fill the sea, the earth will be filled with an awareness of the glory of the LORD."

ISAIAH 2

2 "In the last days, the mountain
of the Lord's house will be the highest of all—
the most important place on earth.
It will be raised above the other hills,
and people from all over the world

will stream there to worship.
3 People from many nations will come and say,
"Come, let us go up to the mountain of the Lord,
to the house of Jacob's God.
There he will teach us his ways,
and we will walk in his paths."
For the Lord's teaching will go out from Zion;
his word will go out from Jerusalem.
4 The Lord will mediate between nations
and will settle international disputes.
They will hammer their swords into plowshares
and their spears into pruning hooks.
Nation will no longer fight against nation,
nor train for war anymore."

ISAIAH 65

25 "The wolf and the lamb will feed together.
The lion will eat hay like a cow.
But the snakes will eat dust.
In those days no one will be hurt or
destroyed on my holy mountain.
I, the Lord, have spoken!"

15 THREE HEBREW MEN - WE WILL NOT BOW

So many people are living as exiles in this day. Borders in many places have disappeared intentionally. To be sure, this tragedy and upheaval has been orchestrated by the cabal. To bring in their New World Order they must destroy languages, cultures, and borders. This criminal mafia has made conditions unbearable politically and financially, worldwide, on purpose.

Undoubtedly, some of the migrants are part of their evil scheme, free to perpetrate lawlessness and mayhem wherever they go, without fear of prosecution. But it is heartbreaking to see so many who have felt the necessity to risk life and limb to leave their homeland. Everyone I have ever talked to, who has left their home country, would go back today if they could. The conditions in their country had become unbearable. Many I know literally fled the cartels in Mexico. The stories they tell would make your hair stand on end. They are living in America as exiles. Maybe you believe they do or don't deserve political asylum. But no matter how you look at it, they felt they **had** to escape their home country and go to a foreign land where they don't know the language or the customs. My heart goes out to them, and it is one of the reasons I work day and night to destroy the New World Order.

I've never had to flee my homeland. I have lived in America all my life. But I feel like the America I knew, is gone. What I see today bears little resemblance to the America I grew up in. When I was a little girl, we sang Christian songs at our public school. We said the Pledge of Allegiance every morning and I felt that everyone meant it. The topics that have become commonplace were never even heard of when I was a little girl. Autism was extremely rare. So was depression. No one questioned their gender. Fathers were respected. I didn't even know anyone whose parents were divorced. It was A-OK to be white. We were proud to be Americans. So in a funny way, I feel a bit like an exile. That thought process was one of my first wake up moments years ago. I was wondering where would we move to, if America was taken over. And the answer was...nowhere.

Now all the verses in the Bible about exiles take on new meaning. The LORD promised in His Word that all the exiles will be brought home. Here's one example:

ZEPHANIAH 3

19 "And I will deal severely with all

who have oppressed you.

I will save the weak and helpless ones;

I will bring together those who were chased away.

I will give glory and fame to my former exiles,

wherever they have been mocked and shamed."

What a wonderful promise. Share that with your friends who miss their homeland. That might even include Americans.

MICAH 4

6 "In that coming day," says the Lord,
"I will gather together those who are lame,
those who have been exiles,
and those whom I have filled with grief.

7 Those who are weak will survive as a remnant;
those who were exiles will become a strong nation.
Then I, the Lord, will rule from Jerusalem
as their king forever."

Imagine, once we remove the cabal, and peace settles over the earth, everyone will be free. Free to live where they please...not just live somewhere because they can't live in their homeland. Every nation will be free. Won't that be wonderful?

That is one of the many beautiful aspects of the Millennial Kingdom of Christ on earth. Yes, there will be nations during the Millennial Kingdom of Christ on earth.

ISAIAH 2

4 *"The Lord will mediate between nations*
and will settle international disputes.
They will hammer their swords into plowshares
and their spears into pruning hooks.
Nation will no longer fight against nation,
nor train for war anymore."

The day of exiles is coming to an end. Praise the LORD!

The reason I'm bringing this up is because I want you to imagine what it must have felt like to be an exile in Babylon. About 500 years before Christ, King Nebuchadnezzar literally hauled the people living in Judea all the way to Babylon.

Everything there was different.

The language was different.

The customs were different.

The religion was different.

The food was different.

The laws were different.

And the exiles had no options.

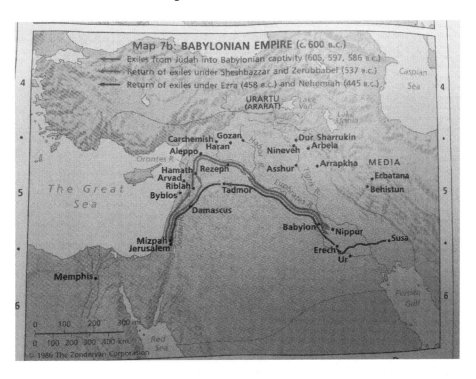

That brings us to the next historical Biblical account that we are fulfilling in our day. It is recorded in the Book of Daniel, Chapter 4, and it is about four exemplary young Hebrew men who were taken into Babylonian captivity. They were committed to honoring the LORD no matter where they lived. No matter who was watching. No matter what the costs. They were true Israelites...not just INOs - Israelites in Name Only.

Those four young men – Daniel, Shadrach, Meschach, and Abednego were part of Judah's royal family and other noble families, and their wisdom came to the attention of the leaders in Babylon. They were brought into special training for royal service to the king.

DANIEL 1

3 "Then the king ordered Ashpenaz, his chief of staff, to bring to the palace some of the young men of Judah's royal family and other noble families, who had been brought to Babylon as captives.

4 "Select only strong, healthy, and good-looking young men," he said. "Make sure they are well versed in every branch of learning, are gifted with knowledge and good judgment, and are suited to serve in the royal palace. Train these young men in the language and literature of Babylon.

5 The king assigned them a daily ration of food and wine from his own kitchens. They were to be trained for three years, and then they would enter the royal service."

They were offered all of the delicacies from the king's own kitchens, which at first blush sounds wonderful. But there is a little bitty problem. The food from the king's table had been banned by the LORD. Since Christ's ascension, he told us to consider those foods clean. (Acts 10:9-16) But at that time, those foods were off limits. One of the reasons for those food restrictions was to help the Israelites stay unified as a people. The culture of foods and clothing and traditions helped them to do that, even when they were in exile. These young men could have made an excuse and accepted the food as required by their captors. But to them, these were not just rules. The food and the clothing and traditions kept them connected to the LORD and to each other, to have strength in their time of suffering. They were determined not to defile themselves, and asked permission to eat their customary food, according to the Law of Moses.

I also wonder if they were concerned that some of the food they were offered was "meat sacrificed to idols"...or even worse. We recoil at the notion. Babylon was a pagan culture, and it wouldn't surprise me if some of this food was human flesh. Either way, these young men were bound and determined not to defile themselves. Surprisingly they gained permission to eat the vegetables and water that the LORD had prescribed.

After the 10-day test, it was noticeable that Daniel, Shadrach, Meschach, and Abednego were stronger and healthier-looking than the rest. So that was the first test of their fortitude against the pressure to conform to the Babylonian culture. These four wise young men had taken their Bible lessons to heart. They had prepared beforehand that if they were asked to do something against their conscience and God's law, they were going to stand and honor the LORD. I imagine they had to stand up against that pagan culture many times.

We don't hear anything else about them until King Nebuchadnezzar built a gigantic statue in his honor, and ordered all the people to gather and bow down upon command. First of all, that sounds ridiculous. What kind of narcissist does that? The same kind that forces people to take a jab or they will lose their job. The same kind that locks people down in their homes with no medical evidence. The same kind that suspends social media accounts of people who say something they disagree with. The same kind that refuses to listen to millions protesting election fraud, and calls them insurrectionists instead. The same kind that says parents have no rights in what their children are taught. That's the kind. Wow...and we were making fun of Nebuchadnezzar!

Just in case anyone had a crazy notion of not obeying King Nebuchadnezzar by bowing down to his statue, there was one itsy bitsy consequence. You would be thrown into a furnace of fire.

Well.

I'm thinking you'd get pretty close to 100% compliance.

"Hey...what gives? What harm can be done if I just bow down. What good am I anyway, to anyone, if I'm burned alive?" I can imagine every excuse in the book. Any excuse will suffice. But the truth is, most people don't need a lot of threats. They will comply without the threats. Why would I say that? I have proof. One hundred fifty million Americans took an experimental "vaccine" without even batting an eye. And got boosted too! Because the authorities said so.

The day came when the people all gathered together for the bowing to Nebuchadnezzar worship service. That's what it was, after all. A worship service for King Nebby.
The statue was there.
The furnace was blazing hot.
The trumpet sounded.
And everyone dropped to their knees.

Everyone except Shadrach, Meshach, and Abednego. (Daniel was in a position of authority, and was not in the crowd.) There they stood. Can you imagine it? You could spot the young men from miles away. In a sea of people with their faces on the ground and their behinds in the air, Shadrach, Meschach, and Abednego stood strong and tall.

The insolence!

The outrage!

Of all people!

These three men had been given special honors to serve the king! How could they repay such kindness by biting the very hand that fed them? But they refused to bow. King Nebuchadnezzar could call them names. He could threaten. But they would not bow. And that was that. Shadrach, Meshach, and Abednego had decided long ago that they would not bow down to an idol. Period. They would only bow to God.

They even said they understood that they could die if they were thrown into the fiery furnace. They also knew the LORD was able to save them from the fiery furnace. But either way, they would not bow down to the idol.

Does that remind anyone of anything that we have been through recently? Only about a million things. The New World Order Cabal expects us to bow down.
Bow down to their mainstream media narrative.
Bow down to their ridiculous waste of our money.
Bow down to the mockery of our Constitutional rights.
Bow down and give up your gun.

Bow down to the election fraud.

Bow down to the jab.

Bow down to the gender insanity.

Bow down to the loss of our borders and our sovereignty.

No.

We will not bow down.

You can threaten us.

You can fire us.

You can mock us.

You can jail us.

You can ban us.

You can cancel our social media accounts entirely.

You can cancel our finance accounts.

You can separate us from our friends and family.

But we will not bow down.

We know the LORD is able to save us and our Country. And we believe that He will. But even if He does not, we will not bow down. Fifty million out of 200 million people in America refused to take the jab. 50 million is a lot of rebels. The New World Order Cabal is piping mad at our insolence. They have tried everything to get us to bow down. They want to throw us in that fiery furnace for not bowing down.

So the record is that they did it. The king of Babylon made an example of these three wonderful young men. They were literally thrown into the fiery furnace and it was even turned up three times hotter! The poor fool who threw them into the furnace actually died because it was so hot. But the LORD was with these young men. The king looked into the furnace and saw the three men walking around in the fiery furnace! How amazing is that?! And not only that, there was a fourth man in the fiery furnace with them! The preincarnate Christ our LORD was with them! He is with us too, Patriots.

And sometimes when we make those strong stands and we feel the heat of their attacks, we sense the LORD'S presence even more. And even though some of us have been through some very difficult and challenging and even heartbreaking trials, we've come through without even being singed. Just like these men, we don't even smell like smoke. And even though some might not admit it, they are inspired by your faith and courage. And one day, as the Word of God says, they will recognize that you were right and the LORD was with you and you heard and followed His voice. Just like those three Hebrew men, Shadrach, Meshach, and Abednego.

The New World Order laughs at the sheep who just believe what they're told and are so asleep that they fall for every trick. But they are not laughing at us. They are afraid of us. That's why they fight us so hard. They don't want the courage we have to stand and not bow, to transfer to the sheep.

That's why they have to fight us so hard, and ridicule us so hard, to cause the sheep to continue to bow. But just like these three men...whether the others bow or whether they stand, we have made the choice.

We will not bow down to the New World Order.

16 DANIEL - WE GOT HIM THIS TIME!

Daniel is one of my absolute favorite heroes from God's Word. In every account of Daniel, he is faithful and shows himself to be an exemplary model of honor and obedience to the LORD. He reminds me of our President. So courageous and willing to stand and do the right thing even when the powerful are bound and determined to destroy him.

Remember the story of Daniel in the lions' den? We are all right now in that lions' den. There are ravenous lions all around us trying to devour us Patriots and all of humanity. And who are the lions trying to devour most? Our wonderful President Trump. President Trump has been in the proverbial lions' den since he came down the golden escalator. They have been trying to find one way or another to destroy him, and just like Daniel, they can't find anything wrong with him! What does that tell us!? He is as clean as a whistle! Pure as the driven snow! If there was one scintilla of anything he had done wrong, they would have sniffed it out after all this time. But these wild, hungry lions haven't. Because it simply doesn't exist.

So why did the governors hate Daniel so much? And why do these political leaders of the cabal hate President Trump so much? For the very same reason. Because they could not get away with their evil with Daniel around. President Trump is our Daniel. He is a threat to their way of doing corrupt business in Washington and all over the world. They know he will put a stop to every evil crime. He will protect the children. He will stop the financial corruption. He will stop judicial corruption. He put an end to wars. During his first term their military industrial complex could not churn out all that money through endless wars. These criminals don't want anyone holding them to an account for their crimes or for anyone to slow them down in their evil plots and schemes. That's why they hated Daniel and that's why they hate President Trump.

The men who hated Daniel couldn't find anything he was doing wrong, as hard as they looked. So they manufactured a crime about Daniel's faith and "called" it a crime. The king foolishly fell into their trap. The evil governors in Daniel's day tricked the king into signing an edict against prayer. Literally no one could pray, except to the king, for 30 days. As soon as Daniel heard the edict that no one could pray for 30 days to anyone except the king, what was the next thing he did? He went to pray. Did he close the door? Nope. Did he close the window? Nope. He prayed just like he always had. With the door wide open and the window wide open toward Jerusalem. Wide open for all to see and hear. What a man of faith. He knew the consequences were that he would be thrown into a den of hungry lions. But that didn't slow him down one half second.

Daniel was truly free. He had decided long ago to honor the LORD in his life. And nothing, I repeat nothing, was going to stop him in that mission. He didn't even consider not fulfilling his vows of prayer. That's our first clue on how to have a successful life of faith like Daniel's. We make our decision to follow the LORD, no matter what. Nothing will get in the way. Of course, the Rinos and Democrats in Babylon were onto Daniel just like that. And immediately when the king heard that they had arrested Daniel, and convicted him of this crime of prayer, he knew the governors had tricked him. These people had no shame. Sadly, even the king could not reverse his own edict, no matter how hard he tried.

I can just imagine the look on the king's face. First in horror that his faithful governor, Daniel, would be thrown into the lions' den because of this dirty trick. And second I can imagine the king's look of disgust at these governors. I can also imagine Daniel's face. Daniel didn't make the king feel any worse than he already felt. Daniel put his trust in the LORD just as Shadrach, Meshach, and Abednego had when they were threatened with being tossed into that fiery furnace.

Doesn't Daniel sound a lot like our wonderful President Trump? They have attacked President Trump continuously and mercilessly. To navigate this minefield of vicious attacks without being convicted is nothing short of a miracle. But that's what President Trump did and continues to do to this very day. Every time they think they've got him, he eludes their grasp. They've never laid a glove on him...even when they stole the election. He just continues to grow stronger and stronger. That is ultimately what they fear the most.

They have threatened him over and over, and made attempts on his life, and called him every name in the book, and ridiculed him all throughout social media. They have banned him from speaking, even during a political campaign, and sued him more times than I can remember. They even stole, literally stole, the 2020 election from him. But he continues to speak the truth about their crimes and he continues to have full confidence that we will make America great again.

Never have we seen even a twinge of fear on his face. Never have we seen the slightest inkling of doubt from him. You always get the idea from President Trump that he has the inside track on what's going on behind the scenes. Nothing can stop what is coming. He says he's "The Chosen One." I would have to agree. No doubt he is the chosen leader to guide us through these crazy times. Literally the Great Awakening, the Battle of Armageddon, the casting out of our enemies, and the 1,000 Years of Peace on earth.

I can just imagine those criminals shrieking with hideous delight at the thought of Daniel being attacked by those lions.

"Hey, this time we've got Daniel! We will finally be rid of him and be able to go back to our crimes full-time!"

How many times have they said, "We've got Trump this time"? And every time, their plan backfires. President Trump just grows in popularity, he is found innocent, and they are exposed for the corrupt criminals they are.

We are all in this den of lions to one degree or another. As President Trump said, they (the NWO cabal) are really after us. He's just standing in the way. I think of the January 6 prisoners and all they're going through in the lions' den. It's bad enough to go to prison, but to be treated unjustly and not even to have a trial is so unfair. Not unlike Daniel. Not unlike President Trump. None of this has been fair. People have lost their jobs over the stupid jab. How unfair. Police officers and firefighters and our wonderful military who have risked their lives, were fired when they refused to take the jab...a jab that had not even been approved and was only under emergency use authorization. The outrage!

We have been censored and spied on by the vicious "intelligence community" and banned for simply speaking the truth on social media! We have tried daily and desperately to save lives and to wake up the masses, only to be thwarted by these ravenous criminals! I could go on and on about how we have fought to protect our children from being taught "LORD knows what" in school, only to be threatened by the Department of Justice. We've had our elections stolen from us when it was obvious that President Trump won. It was obvious that Kari Lake won. It has been obvious that these machines are intentionally fraudulent and being used to steal our elections and all our rights under the Constitution of the United States of America. I could go on and on and on about how it's all been unfair. But you know all of that.

We are in that den of hungry, ravenous lions.

But...somehow, by a miracle, we are safe.

It's a long night.

We see their sharp teeth catching the moonlight.

We hear their purring and feel their hot breath, but here we sit.

We are fine.

We might not sleep a wink.

But we know that morning is coming when we will be set free and come out of this lions' den.

The story of Daniel in the lions' den is epic. When the king asked Daniel if his God saved him, Daniel gave honor to the LORD and said,

DANIEL 6

21 "Daniel answered, "Long live the king!

22 My God sent his angel to shut the lions' mouths so that they would not hurt me, for I have been found innocent in his sight. And I have not wronged you, Your Majesty."

The Lord shut their claws too! There wasn't a scratch on Daniel. What a testimony of faith and the loving-kindness of the LORD!

You know the rest of the story. The king had those evil conniving governors who railroaded Daniel, thrown into the lions' den, along with their wives and children! The Bible says they were torn to ribbons before they even touched the ground. That's what will happen, my friends, to the hateful, ruthless, evil, satan worshiping New World Order cabal that has done untold damage to each one of us.

This miracle was unmistakable evidence of the True and Living God and His love for Daniel. To witness this miracle and Daniel's confident faith in the LORD was life-changing for King Darius. He sent out an edict for his entire kingdom to worship the God of Daniel.

WOW.

This transformation didn't happen overnight. After Daniel and the other Israelites were taken captive to Babylon, we begin to see that society moving step-by-step to becoming a culture of faith. Imagine your life...even your suffering...being used to turn an entire nation to the LORD.

WOW.

Actually, I think it will. I think once all this truth comes out, and everyone realizes how we fought for them, even though we were treated unfairly and cruelly, it will have a powerful impact. The entire world will have experienced genuine love and undeniable faith in action.

That's where we're headed as humanity. Once we toss these criminals into the lions' den, all the world will know that the LORD is true. And His Word is true. The world will know that the criminal mafia NWO was the actual Beast of Revelation and that we have defeated them in the Great Battle of Armageddon.

This is Biblical.

After that, the earth will be filled with the knowledge of the LORD as the waters fill the sea, and everyone will worship the God of Daniel.

17 ESTHER - THE QUEEN WHO SAVED THE WORLD

Once upon a time there was a beautiful young girl who lived in a little town in a faraway land. Her life took a dramatic turn when she was chosen to enter a beauty contest.

The prize?

To be Queen of the World.

Seriously.

Her name was Hadassah.

But to hide her Hebrew ethnicity, her name was changed to Esther.

If you're thinking God must have had a plan, you'd be right.

This is yet another historical account of how the LORD placed His chosen warrior in a position of influence, to save the world.

If this was a fairy tale I'd tell you Esther became the queen of the land and she and the king lived happily ever after. The end. But there's actually a lot more to the story and how it is being reenacted in our day. This is how Esther was chosen by the LORD, as we have been, "for such a time as this" to risk our lives and to save humanity. How's that for a modern-day fulfillment to an ancient historical account from the Bible?

Yes, Esther was chosen by the king to be his queen. She was a poor little orphan girl, who had been adopted by her cousin, Mordecai. Actually, being chosen by the king was not quite as glamorous as a fairy-tale, in my opinion. The king could do whatever he pleased, and he did.

His name was Xerxes, also known as Ahasuerus. I guess they

called him Xerxes, because no one could say Ahasuerus.

It was dangerous to be a queen back in the day. Something very mysterious happened to Xerxes' first queen when she refused to be paraded around in front of the kingdom's big shots at one of their drunken "parties."

Not to worry. The king's counselors convinced him to have a kingdom-wide beauty contest and take the most beautiful girls into the king's harem. The auditioning was a one-on-one performance, if you know what I mean. And if you were not chosen to be queen, you spent the rest of your life as a spinster. Lovely.

Esther was not only beautiful, she had exemplary character beyond her years. From what we know of Esther, she trusted the LORD and always sought His guidance through prayer. The LORD guided her to humbly ask for and follow the advice of those who knew the king's preferences. All the beauty contest participants were primped and waxed and buffed and beautified for weeks, before the "audition." Turns out the advice Esther heeded paid off! Xerxes chose Esther for her beauty and her grace...she was exactly what he was looking for! Esther was crowned and given a grand royal reception befitting a Queen. Esther's life of prayer and trust in the LORD would come in handy.

It appears that after the coronation, Xerxes shuffled Esther to the side until the he required her services, and for official functions. She had to forgo a normal marriage and children and a little thing called true love. But, at least she wasn't wasting away in the harem. This was her lot and she accepted it, gracefully. Truth be told, there were not many fine lots to be had in the Kingdom of Persia, unless you were one of the wealthy and powerful elite. So most accepted their lot as best they could.

Which brings up an interesting point. The Book of Esther is the basis for the Biblical springtime celebration called Purim, which means "casting lots." That is basically "rolling the dice" and that comes later in the story. It's also about each of us having a "lot" in life that the LORD has assigned to each one of us, to fulfill the role He wants each of us to play in this grand plan to save humanity. Esther accepted and played her role beautifully.

Esther had a cousin named Mordecai who was also a man of strong faith. Interestingly, years before the beauty contest, he discovered and reported an assassination plot against the king and saved the king's life. Mordecai was never rewarded, but he didn't mind. He wasn't reporting the plot for a reward. When Hadassah (Esther) was taken to the harem, Mordecai wisely told her not mention she was a Hebrew. He knew the political climate and felt it best to keep that little tidbit quiet. I guess now would be a good time to mention that I think Esther symbolizes the chosen warriors in this battle of Armageddon. Just like her, we are the scattered tribes of Israel, either by birth or by adoption. We have the same faith in God as Esther did, and undoubtedly we have been chosen "for such as time as this."

As in all great tales, there is an evil villain. In this one, his name is Haman. I've always called him Hateful Haman because he hated anyone who would not bow down to him. Guess who Hateful Haman represents? The New World Order cabal, of course! They expect everyone to do whatever they say. They consider themselves to be the authority and if someone does not bow, there **will** be consequences!

Guess who refused to bow to Hateful Haman when he was paraded through the streets? God-fearing Mordecai...of course. So true to form, Hateful Haman made the only reasonable decision. He devised a plot to destroy each and every Hebrew in the entire kingdom of Persia! Now you know why I call him Hateful Haman! Of course that's what evil villains do. Hateful, despicable, terrifying crimes against humanity for no reason! That's why Hateful Haman represents the New World Order in the Book of Esther. And since Haman was a close confidant of

King Xerxes, he made up a terrible lie that the Hebrew people were lazy good-for-nothings and traitors to the kingdom. He told King Xerxes the Hebrews should be done away with. Sadly, King Xerxes trusted Haman, and he was probably distracted doing something else, and agreed to have all the Hebrews killed. He couldn't allow lazy traitors in his kingdom, after all! Foolish kings listen to creeps like Hateful Haman.

Even if we don't technically have a "king," sadly many government leaders have assumed the authority as a king, and daily deny us our human rights. The mandatory Covid jab is a prime example of signing lives away with a stroke of a pen. Hateful Haman cast lots to determine the date of the execution of every Hebrew man, woman, and child in the Persian Empire. Xerxes had the edict sent out that very day!

FYI.

King's edicts cannot be reversed.

Oh no.

I don't have to tell you that the New World Order cabal has sent out countless edicts for the destruction of God's people, all over the world. They have edicts to destroy our health, to destroy our livelihoods, to destroy our currency, to destroy our families, to destroy our peace, to destroy our gender identity, to destroy our sanity, to destroy our very faith. The Covid debacle is an edict for the destruction of humanity that would even make Xerxes cringe.

Mordecai read the edict and was beside himself with grief. He wore burlap to show his grief and was in bitter tears. The people had no Second Amendment in that day and couldn't even defend themselves! Guess who had no idea any of this going on? Little Esther in her ivory tower! Her attendants didn't bother her with something so trivial as the king signing an edict to kill all the Hebrews in the kingdom. Mordecai somehow got the news to her. She was horrified, but she didn't know what she could do to help. The edict had already been sent out and could not be reversed. And besides that, she only went to the king when she was summoned. If she went to the king without being summoned, she would likely meet the same fate as the last queen! Esther didn't know what she could do.

We might feel the same way. What can I do? I'm just one person. The New World Order already has these evil plans in motion. They have already sent out the unwitting jab henchmen, and have mainstream media and social media blasting out the NWO narrative. Plus, I could lose friends and family and my job if I speak out!

The famous response from Mordecai was this.

ESTHER 4

14 "If you keep quiet at a time like this, deliverance and relief for the Jews will arise from some other place, but you and your relatives will die. Who knows if perhaps you were made queen **for just such a time as this?"**

So let me stop right there.

We are Esther.

We have been put in this position where we know what is going on, and we have been given specific instructions to fight in this battle by exposing the truth, <u>for such a time as this.</u>

Specifically "for such a time as this"...is this Great Battle of Armageddon! Just like Esther trying to save all the Hebrews in the Persian Empire, we are trying desperately to rescue humanity...from the jab, from the financial disaster, from the gender disaster, from the depopulation disaster, from the trafficking disaster, from the education disaster, from every disaster the New World Order has cooked up. This is our role in this day. Sometimes it seems daunting and frightening. Sometimes we risk the loss of money and reputation and jobs and family and friends. But our response is similar to Esther's:

ESTHER 4

16 "Go and gather together all the Jews of Susa and fast for me. Do not eat or drink for three days, night or day. My maids and I will do the same. And then, though it is against the law, I will go in to see the king. If I must die, I must die."

Here was the plan.
Pray.
Simple as that.
Pray.
For three days fast and pray.
No water.
No food.
For three days pray only.
That was the plan.

What is so wonderful is that when we pray, somehow, the LORD sets the wheels in motion so the prayers are answered. And we step into the answer one step at a time...by faith. We don't need to necessarily see the next step ahead. After three days of the entire kingdom of Hebrews praying and fasting, Esther knew exactly what the LORD wanted her to do.

She would go to the king and bow humbly. And if her head was still on her shoulders, she would ask him to come to dinner!

How do you like that for a plan?

Simple.

Genius.

Do you see?

When you're king, people are coming to you all the time asking for this, asking for that, pleading and begging and never asking what the **king** might want. So Esther wisely asked him to dinner. But it was not just any dinner. It was a veritable feast. She put on the whole dog. She spared no expense and made a fabulous spread. The best delicacies with all of his favorites.

Beautifully decorated, just the way he liked it. I'm sure she had entertainment that she knew he would enjoy. Remember, Esther learned well what the king liked.

By the way, she also invited Hateful Haman...just as the LORD directed her to. After that fine dinner, the king asked Esther what she needed. Obviously, Esther had not risked her life just to serve him dinner.

"So my beautiful, delightful Queen, what do you need?"

This was Esther's chance!

Tell him, Esther!

You've got the king all buttered up!

You've got him right where you want him!

Tell him, Esther, that Hateful Haman wants to kill all the Hebrews!

But Esther didn't do that.

Most of us would've done that! That's what happens in many of the movies about Esther. But that is NOT what happened in real life. (I hate it when movies do that.)

The LORD had put on Esther's heart not just to invite him to **one** fabulous dinner, but to invite him to **two** fabulous dinners, and to wait to tell him her request afterward.

It makes sense.

Her request was a big deal.

She wanted the request to make the biggest impact.

And she wanted the king to feel like he was treated like a king!

No one wants to feel like they are just being used...especially a king.

She might not have known why the LORD put it on her heart to wait to make her request at the second dinner, but she was going to follow His prompting and trust the plan. Period.

She refused to listen to worrying thoughts, like "What if the king doesn't come to the second dinner! The plan will fail!"

Or "What if Haman goes through with his evil plan early?"

Esther refused to worry. She refused to fear. She simply trusted the LORD was leading her and followed His prompting by faith.

Does that sound familiar? This journey of the Great Awakening has had so many twists and turns. I'm so glad that we've been together in the Freedom Force Battalion to pray and to follow the LORD'S promptings on our hearts, and to do whatever He assigns for us to do. We trust the plan, and refuse to worry or fear. Period.

Esther had no way of knowing that on that very night after her beautiful banquet, the king would not be able to sleep. I wonder if she put something in the knockwurst that kept him up all night.

What does a king do when he can't sleep?

He couldn't watch TV.

He couldn't play video games.

Of all things, God put it on his mind to call the historian!

A historian!

Of all things!

I guess he figured that would put him to sleep!

What an answer to prayer!

And get this! The historian turned right to the page where Mordecai saved the king's life from the assassination plot!

How great is that!

Don't tell me that's not the LORD'S answer to prayer!

The LORD is so amazing!

It is so fun to trust the plan and watch it unfold!

Remember that, when some crazy news comes on the TV.

Trust the plan.

This is not just a human plan.

This is the LORD'S plan to rescue humanity.

No doubt about it.

So the king finally went to sleep, thinking about how he would reward Mordecai. He decided to ask Haman in the morning. You're going to need more popcorn, because at that very same moment, Haman was devising his evil plan to kill Mordecai. See how the LORD was at work in answer to the Israelites' prayers? As we pray, the LORD is tripping up all these creepy criminals, and every evil plot they scheme backfires on them!

That very morning Haman got up extra early and installed a huge sharp pole on which to execute Mordecai, because he couldn't wait for the edict execution date to arrive! Haman was out of control! Mordecai was square in Haman's crosshairs, but he still refused to bow to Haman. Just like we will not bow down to the New World Order.

We will not bow.

No.

We will not wear your masks.

We will not take your vaccine.

We will not believe your fake news.

We will not stop exposing your crimes.

We will not fill in the blank.

We don't care if you threaten us.

We will not bow.

We are cut out of the same cloth as Mordecai!

We will not bow!

The very evil that Haman plotted for righteous Mordecai, was going to happen to him! Boomerang! Just watch and see!

Hateful Haman had no idea God's people had been fasting and praying.

Haman had no idea the king had been up that night, and had discovered how Mordecai saved his life.

Haman had no idea the LORD put on the king's heart to reward Mordecai.

So when the king asked Haman for ideas on how to reward a faithful servant, **Hateful Haman thought the king was talking about rewarding him!** Of course he would! What a narcissist! So of course, Haman told the king a great reward would be where the honoree would be paraded through the town, to receive the adoration of the people. Just imagine the look on Haman's face when King Xerxes agreed to his idea, and ordered him to parade his mortal enemy, Mordecai, through the streets of Persia! The LORD is hilarious!

After Hateful Haman literally paraded Mordecai through the streets giving him honor from the king, he knew that the lots were not being cast in his favor. The New World Order knows the very same thing. They've been running the world for all these years and all of the sudden, they are losing power! They can see that the LORD is giving us honor and that the tide has turned in our favor. The righteous will begin to rule and they know it! The criminals at the top of the cabal actually know the Word of God really well. They have no choice but to move forward, inching step by step by step closer to their demise. Just like Hateful Haman.

Haman was in a foul mood, even for him, but he went to Esther's party for the king anyway. That was the last party he would ever go to. Because at that party, after Esther pulled out all the stops, the king asked again, "What would you like for me to do for you? Up to half of my kingdom!"

And that's when she said it.

ESTHER 7

2 "On this second occasion, while they were drinking wine, the king again said to Esther, "Tell me what you want, Queen Esther. What is your request? I will give it to you, even if it is half the kingdom!"

3 Queen Esther replied, "If I have found favor with the king, and if it pleases the king to grant my request, I ask that my life and the lives of my people will be spared.

4 For my people and I have been sold to those who would kill, slaughter, and annihilate us. If we had merely been sold as slaves, I could remain quiet, for that would be too trivial a matter to warrant disturbing the king."

5 "Who would do such a thing?" King Xerxes demanded. "Who would be so presumptuous as to touch you?"

6 Esther replied, "This wicked Haman is our adversary and our enemy." Haman grew pale with fright before the king and queen.

7 Then the king jumped to his feet in a rage and went out into the palace garden."

8 In despair he fell on the couch where Queen Esther was reclining, just as the king was returning from the palace garden. The king exclaimed, "Will he even assault the queen right here in the palace, before my very eyes?" And as soon as the king spoke, his attendants covered Haman's face, signaling his doom.

9 Then Harbona, one of the king's eunuchs, said, "Haman has set up a sharpened pole that stands seventy-five feet tall in his own courtyard. He intended to use it to impale Mordecai, the man who saved the king from assassination."

"Then impale Haman on it!" the king ordered.

10 So they impaled Haman on the pole he had set up for Mordecai, and the king's anger subsided."

Haman knew the lot had fallen to him and this was his end.

Begging on Esther's lap didn't help. Of course, Haman never offered anyone mercy, so he received none. The king had hateful Haman impaled on the very skewer he had prepared for Mordecai. And THAT was the end of Hateful Haman.

The New World Order cabal has plotted our demise...whether it was FEMA camps, or bioweapons, or financial devastation, or nuclear holocaust, or war, or rampant crime. They have literally joined in league with the demons to plot our destruction. But whatever they have plotted for us...whatever pit they have dug for us, the LORD says THEY will fall into. No doubt about it.

The Book of Esther is really the story of reversing Agenda 21, and the Destruction of the NWO!

Esther and the Hebrews had just one more eensy weensy problem. The king had already proclaimed an edict for all the Hebrews to be killed. He couldn't reverse the edict. That is like the evil plots the New World Order and their minions have set in motion to destroy humanity. Their evil plans can't be reversed.

But the king could proclaim another edict.

Guess what the second edict was! It was the Second Amendment! It was the Right to Bear Arms! This edict allowed God's people to fight back to protect themselves. And that's exactly what they did. They made weapons. A LOT of them.

Our forefathers knew the history of the Israelites fighting back. They knew that tyrants never change. And they knew the Bible and the truth about End Times. That's why they made sure we had the Right To Bear Arms. That is why America still has not fallen and will not fall. The Right To Bear Arms is the one right that protects all our other rights.

Because of that right, we fight back every day and protect ourselves by exposing their crimes. Exposing the lies. Exposing the truth.

Do you want to know how it turned out? Do you want know if the Israelites were able to overcome the edict for their execution?

Oh yes! Boy did they!

Israelites destroyed so many of their enemies that the king put out another edict that they could have another day to kill more of their enemies who came to kill them! So, not only were the Israelites not killed, they were able to destroy all the Hateful Hamans throughout the entire kingdom. Well isn't that a fine lot! The Israelites didn't just sit around waiting for someone else to save them. They were given the right to the tools of their own deliverance!

Just as the LORD promised, and I say over and over, we will rule and reign with Him. That's exactly what happened after the Israelites' great victory. King Xerxes raised Mordecai, and others like Mordecai, into positions of authority, who ruled and reigned in the kingdom! That is where all of humanity is headed!

HAMAN WAS EXECUTED AND MORDECAI BECAME A GOVERNOR.

Now you know that Esther is not some stale old historical account of people you don't know or care about. The story of Esther is about us defeating the New World Order! The LORD has ordained that we have the weapons to defeat our enemies. Yes that may mean guns. But more importantly we wage this Battle of Armageddon with truth bullets!

2nd CORINTHIANS 10

3 "We are human, but we don't wage war as humans do.

4 We use God's mighty weapons, not worldly weapons, to knock down the strongholds of human reasoning and to destroy false arguments.

5 We destroy every proud obstacle that keeps people from

knowing God. We capture their rebellious thoughts and teach them to obey Christ.

6 And after you have become fully obedient, we will punish everyone who remains disobedient."

We aren't marching in the streets.

We aren't burning things down.

But make no mistake.

We are destroying the NWO cabal.

Our weapon is the truth.

The truth is a mighty weapon to knock down the strongholds!

They could stop us if we were waging a human war.

But they can't stop the truth.

The truth is an unstoppable force.

All we have to do is tell it.

Nothing can stop what is coming.

One more thing.

The historical account of Queen Esther is quite unique. The world was saved by a "Queen." Hmmm. For those who have been fighting in the Freedom Force Battalion as citizen researchers and journalists, does that remind you of anything? Maybe the "Queen of Heaven?" Also known as the "Woman in Labor." Also known as the "Sign of the Son of Man." I almost missed it!

God's Word has been pointing us to this day when the "Queen" would appear and the world would be saved! The Bible has two other names for the "Queen." The Old Testament calls her the "Woman in Labor" and mentions her over and over again. And our LORD Jesus called the "Queen" the "Sign of the Son of Man." He told us in Matthew Chapter 24 that major changes would occur when we saw the "Sign of the Son of Man."

These three things would occur. All the earth would mourn. We would see the Son of Man coming into power. He would gather

His chosen ones from the four corners of the earth...to fight this Great Battle of Armageddon. I go into more detail on the "Queen" in my other books, *"End Times – Major Clues from Minor Prophets"* and *"End Times and 1000 Years of Peace."* The sign our LORD Jesus told us to watch for is delineated here:

REVELATION 12:1-2

1 "Then I witnessed in heaven an event of great significance. I saw a woman clothed with the sun, with the moon beneath her feet, and a crown of twelve stars on her head. 2 She was pregnant, and she cried out because of her labor pains and the agony of giving birth."

Ladies and gentlemen, I have wonderful news to tell you. We have seen this sign.

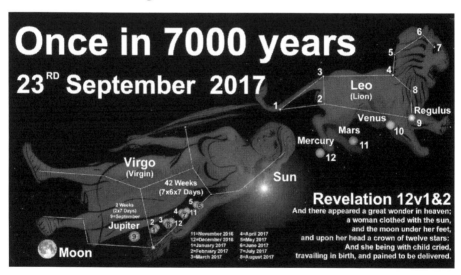

This amazing sign appeared September 23rd, 2017, precisely as John described in The Revelation. And all those major changes our LORD Jesus told us would happen, HAVE HAPPENED. And, even more remarkably, the sign actually began in motion when Jupiter (Melchizedek) entered the "womb" of the "Queen" 42 weeks before. That date was November 8, 2016, and just so happened to be the very same date Donald J. Trump was elected President of the United States of America.

This.   Is.   Biblical.

EPILOGUE

Now do you believe me?!

I know. I know. You believed me before. But now you really do, right? Every Bible story is playing out before our very eyes! Who knew the LORD was going to give us this beautiful road map?

We are going to see the cabal washed away!

We are going to see the promise to Jacob fulfilled!

We're going to see the Omer-ica save the world!

We're going to see the New World order Cabal drowned in the Red Sea and us safely in the Promised Land!

We're going to see law and order all over the world and the fall of the Cabal Canaanite cannibals!

We will drive a stake through the skull of our enemies, so they can never harm us again!

We are watching our enemies destroy each other just like Gideon did. And soon we will witness their complete annihilation!

We will pull down this whole corrupt, diseased temple down on their heads!

We will slay this Goliath NWO monstrosity that has ruled the world!

No more will we have prophets for profit!

We will praise the LORD like Jehoshaphat as we gather the plunder and celebrate and celebrate and celebrate some more!

There won't be one priest of Baal or priest of Asherah left on earth!

The righteous will rule this world like Josiah did, so there will be peace on earth!

No matter how long it takes until we see this victory, we will not bow, just like Shadrach, Meshach, and Abednego refused to bow.

The LORD is with us.

He really is.

And those who prepared a lions' den for us will be thrown into that lions' den. Those who prepared a scaffold for us will end up in judgment on those gallows.

The rest of us will have peace on earth for 1,000 years. His Kingdom come and His will be done on earth as it is in heaven...just as our LORD Jesus told us to pray.

Like Esther, the LORD put us here in these positions "for such a time as this," and no matter what happens, we will remember the promises and the beautiful road map the LORD laid out for us. We refuse to fear or worry. We will, by God's grace, stand still, just as our ancestors did, and see the salvation of the LORD. He set this amazing plan in motion long, long ago and it will be fulfilled. His Kingdom WILL come. And His will WILL be done on earth as it is in Heaven. That is why nothing can stop what is coming.

If you enjoyed connecting the current events in the light of God's Word, you will also enjoy my other books on End Times.

The Revelation decode is called *"End Times and 1000 Years of Peace."* Seriously. I expose the Hollywood and Deep Church deceptions, and explain what the Revelation and End Times prophecies REALLY mean.

And in *"End Times – Major Clues from Minor Prophets"* I show unmistakably where the Minor Prophets foretold about this Great Awakening, this Battle of Good versus evil, and the Kingdom of Christ being established on earth. What a day we are witnessing!

Come join us on *FreedomForce.LIVE* and all our social media where we take the Kingdom of Christ by force!

Made in the USA
Columbia, SC
01 September 2023

22371584R00115